The
Out of Room
Experience

Based on: *The Forgotten Notes*

James J. Mattingly

WestBow
PRESS
A DIVISION OF THOMAS NELSON

WestBow Press books may be ordered through booksellers or by contacting:

WestBow Press
A Division of Thomas Nelson
1663 Liberty Drive
Bloomington, IN 47403
www.westbowpress.com
1-(866) 928-1240

ISBN: 978-1-4497-4536-3 (hc)
ISBN: 978-1-4497-4537-0 (sc)
ISBN: 978-1-4497-4538-7 (e)

Library of Congress Control Number: 2012905449

Printed in the United States of America

WestBow Press rev. date: 10/25/2012

Contents

"I want to someday soon finish
The Out-of-Room Experience
and record it officially and clearly to dedicate it to
my two sisters."
Book #3, p. 81, September 18, 2004

God,
I ain't going to be the fool that lets me
take you away from me!
Book #1 p. 73, March 6, 2003

Preface

Despite what it may appear to be, this book is not an inspirational, informative, or directional text. It's simply an account of what I've called my *Out-of-Room Experience*. And if you find yourself touched, inspired, or even interested, that's excellent. I care about your opinion but I didn't ask for it, nor did you ask anything of me. I simply imposed the story of my life on the general public as if it will further my sense of liberation and fulfill whatever goal I'm currently pursuing.

This is an I-me-my book written by a self-centered mind. So yes, I'll admit, I do wish to woo the world with my extravagant thoughts. But I just wrote the book and you picked it up so you can just as easily put it down. In other words, I won't know if you like it or even read it at all. But that's okay because, despite my desires, I can't expect everyone to be interested. And for those of you who are, I hope you appreciate the story because it's an outpouring of my soul.

The unfortunate thing about this book is that its potential audience is much larger than those who'll understand it. That's a challenge. But you've made it this far (one page), so why stop now? After all, most stories are best understood when they've been read completely.

And to be more blunt, I think for most of you this book will solidify whatever outlook on life you're already committed to. In other words, because of the book's philosophical and religious nature, I think it will either support your preestablished religiosity or support your preestablished distaste for it. And if you find yourself judging it or relating to it, that's fine. After all, it is a story about our humanness, which most of you have experience with, so go ahead and compare if you dare, but be careful.

So I don't intend to relay any words of wisdom that I may have accidentally stumbled upon, nor will I pretend to have an extraordinarily keen awareness of truth. This book will, on the other hand, expose the obsession I had in formulating truths, whether they were good, bad, successful, or unsuccessful. To be a bit more vague, I might even banter my book by saying that its formula is based mostly on confusion, which, to fashion the room experience, is precisely what brought me there.

Furthermore, I don't claim that the formation of this mental room is a universally experienced phenomenon, as is confusion. Even if it was, I wouldn't provide direction on how to get out of it since I'm aware of our obvious differences. I do tell, however, how I myself am still getting out and how the love of God and other people is responsible for my escape.

In sum, the majority of what follows is my poor attempt at developing the mystical lifestyle that I so ambitiously sought to discover, as if the task of creating personal character and identity was entirely mine. And at the height of my despair, it all came down to the illusion of control and the lack of virtue, in which both become reversed by the book's end, completing the tale of my everlasting *Out-of-Room Experience.*

Introduction

About a year ago, I embarked upon the arduous task of reading all 544 pages from my previously written journals (nine books in nine years; 5-1-1999 to 2-13-2008), followed by a typed ten-page paper summarizing them, for the assigned project was to "reflect on ourselves as a writer."

While rereading all the notes, I recalled how passionate and introspective I was. Dozens of thoughts flooded my mind as to how I should introduce myself to the class because, after all, everyone wants to be recognized for something somehow. In my third journal, I said, whoever we are, "We all want purpose; we all want to represent something. Even if it's nothing, that's still something[1]."

After four drafts in one week, the English composition assignment was finished. Following this grade A paper was the inspiration I needed to write this long-awaited book based on those nine journals, which I had previously named *The Forgotten Notes.*

The contents I found in those nine books were prayers and requests to God and expressions of my longings for happiness. But the majority of the passages are best described as my state of mind in the form of existential thoughts.

---

[1]   Book #3, p. 79, 9-14-04.

It's been almost four years since I've written in *The Forgotten Notes,* and I view that as a good thing by its indication of how much more time I've been spending with other people and thus being *outside myself* or outside of room. Writing this book, however, will draw me back in for a short while, which I believe to be just fine as long as it doesn't disturb my responsibilities and personal relationships. In spite of that possibility, I should mention that writing itself was never the problem; it was what I wrote about, how I felt, and what I ignored that eventually brought me to despair.

I was always very spiritual. I thought and wrote deeply about supernatural things. But again, I'm not condoning those acts because I now believe it's healthy to think and write. This book, however, is a story about how, for me, thinking and writing became a deadly combination that eventually, as seen in the last two chapters, changed into a curing combination.

But until then, what follows is based on my past thoughts and beliefs, which spawned the formation of this immaterial room. I'll describe what the room is, what it was like to live in it, and only a small section on the cause of its alleged existence. You'll be reading an assortment of recorded experiences taken out of the order in which they were written—a real story taking place over a nine-year period. This will be accomplished by the inserted passages from *The Forgotten Notes* and today's reflections on them. Today's reflections, indicated by their footnotes, are a sort of narration describing the journal passages. Basically, this book is a combination of thoughts that passionately reminisce on the wonders of life, our basic human experiences seen through the lens of my own microscope.

No journal passages themselves are independent, leaving the interpretation up to you as if I'm some sort of poet or new age prophet. So reading between the lines will hardly be necessary. However, understanding the lines is a different story. But it should help to know that the journal passages chosen for this book are both dependent on one another and dependent on their present-day reflections. Each passage offers a significant contribution toward describing my out-of-room experience. The meaning relayed by these *Forgotten Notes*, however, must be expressed out of chronological order which is also indicated by their footnotes. So again, the passages and their reflections will be combined with quotes from other authors, and all will be carefully put together as pieces of a puzzle to describe my room experience in their own special order.

I found it more effective to describe the analogy of the room prior to what actually led me to it, allowing it to be defined first (chapter one) and exemplified later. But for now, I'll define the room as that safe place produced by my mind in which I escaped to avoid discomfort, to selfishly leave reality in its entirety because of how poorly I felt within it. And you'll see that this was no simple escape. It was not a sick day or a vacation but rather a sort of implanted duty to flee the reality that so effortlessly sneezed in my face.

After writing book number five of *The Forgotten Notes*, I read St. Augustine's *Confessions*. I've inserted a few passages from him because I admire his abstract style of writing as he communicates to God. All of his writing, including the following passage, involves an insightful honesty, which I was surprised to find my own journals taking after. He says,

> Many years—perhaps twelve—had flowed away (and my life with them) since in my 19th year I had been stirred up to a zeal for wisdom instead . . . But

I had spent my young manhood in extreme misery; in such misery I had besought you, on the very brink of manhood, to give me chastity: "Grant me chastity and continence," I had said, "but please, not yet." I was afraid that you would swiftly answer my prayer and swiftly heal me from the sickness of concupiscence, which I would rather have satiated than extinguished. Moreover, I had walked the crooked paths of an impious superstition; not indeed certain of it, but holding it preferable to other things, which I did not seek with due piety, but had fought as an enemy.[2]

St. Augustine would normally refer to Satan as the enemy, contrary to Screwtape who refers to God as the enemy. C. S. Lewis's book titled *The Screwtape Letters* is a majestic work of art intended to be read through the eyes of a demon named Screwtape as he writes to his demon nephew Wormwood. The point of his book is to understand the possible intentions and activities of such horrid beings. Screwtape sometimes refers to Satan as "Our Father," given his perspective of being a demon in hell.

Other such authors, such as Thomas Merton, John Eldredge, and Robert Bly, have given me the tools to more aptly describe *The Out-of-Room Experience*.

Merton's following passage, despite its focus on psychosis, contains the sum of what the remainder of this book entails.

---

[2]   *Confessions* Book 6, 6-10-17.

Excursions into the recollected darkness of contemplation are tempting to anyone with a schizoid character, because it is easy to mistake schizoid withdrawal for contemplative recollection. And a few formulas of contemplative jargon may offer themselves as fatally convenient opportunities for rationalization by one who is merely escaping, within himself, from external reality.[3]

I mistook withdrawing into an abyss of despair, as you will see, for contemplative recollection. These mistaken "fatally convenient opportunities" are conditions which Screwtape tells his nephew to take advantage of:

Keep his mind on the inner life. He thinks his conversion is something *inside* him and his attention is therefore chiefly turned at present to the states of his own mind—or rather to that very expurgated version of them which is all you should allow him to see.[4]

So we enter into . . .

---

[3]   *Thoughts in Solitude*, p. 111.

[4]   *The Screwtape Letters,* p. 11.

1

The Analogical Room

Imagine yourself locked in an actual room. You're alone, hungry, angry, and scared. To survive, you must escape. So begins your search of the room for tools that might help you get out—perhaps a skinny object to slide through the lock or a heavy object with which to smash the window glass. The resources you would need to exit that real room symbolize the immaterial resources needed to exit an immaterial room—the room I created and inhabited for years.

My exit from that immaterial room involved the resources of hope and love. I still occasionally open the door to step back inside, but I always turn back around after remembering the reasons I left.

We all escape to a place inside ourselves. All of us, as a result of stress or discomfort, have made an attempt to somehow escape life. Everyone needs time off to relax and unwind. People daydream, take a day off work, relax, or watch TV. Those positive escapes or vacations are healthy and productive. But the room I created was neither healthy nor productive. It was a superficial, secret place inside myself that deceitfully purported to provide the peace and love I needed.

In the end, it was what I now think of as an abusive vacation in which time away was negative.

Merton says that vacation or solitude "does not mean constantly travelling from one geographical possibility to another."[1] Think about that for a moment. What does it mean to escape or take time away without physically moving? Strictly speaking, to take time away is to reduce the amount of time spent living. It is to reduce the number of opportunities to follow that which is good.

Difficulties are inevitable, no matter who we are. This book describes how I handled these difficulties, but more specifically how I escaped from them.

In book number five, I thought the following:

> Escapism: does such a thing exist? According to me it does. To cease existing is often a desire of mine. Though I am unhappy with that. It is an unhappy reality because I have trouble handling reality for long periods of time; 4+ hours is too much. How to become adjusted to it, I don't know. It will happen someday, but to remain in reality is unattractive.[2]

"To remain in reality is unattractive"? This negative escape was a deliberate mental avoidance of reality and its responsibilities. It begged for an ignorance of what was real, simply because reality was difficult. In this sense, I define *ignorance* as "actively trying to deny the real" or "actively

---

[1]   *Thoughts in Solitude*, p. 77.

[2]   Book #5, p. 21, 2-3-05.

avoiding reality." Naturally, because of the challenge involved with pursuing peace, love, and happiness, my escape from them was directed at finding an easier lifestyle.

My reason for escaping the challenging truths of life was originally to avoid hardship and to be at peace. I soon became discouraged, however, because avoiding hardship was too difficult. It then became even easier to avoid the pursuit of peace altogether by preferring the solace of confusion. My passion for an intense awareness of the good became redirected to the not so good, a sort of rebellion.

Escaping reality can be likened to the avoidance of paying off debt; they both mature into a burden. Initially, it's nice not having to give the lender any money. The first payment is skipped for lack of funds. The second payment is skipped because the first incurred a relaxed penalty and resulted in extra spending money. The third payment is skipped because the borrower begins to think, *Why should I pay? It's my money!*

———

Throughout this book, *the room* will appear to be a physical place. Sometimes it will appear as a sort of demonic being. Tarek Saab, in his book *Gut Check*, writes about *confronting love work & manhood in your twenties.* My room analogy is comparable to Saab's way of describing *pride* when he says it has "a want."

> "Humility doesn't tolerate lying—it demands honesty. In the honest assessment of how I've become successful, pride doesn't want me to

know that I've rarely achieved anything entirely on my own."[3]

During my stay in the room, I was intensely preoccupied with supernatural and abstract concepts, most of which involved the perception of demons, myself, God, and the relationships among those three. This brings us to the drama of my negative escape, which I classify as *habitually denying the good.*

By habitually denying the good, I confused myself, became disconnected from reality, and claimed to be locked in this immaterial room. The following is a confusing passage, but I think it helps describe the rhetorical antics of the room.

> The death of my soul, as well as anyone's soul, would come after a constant preoccupation with that which distracts me from idling, let alone growing in holiness. There is such a mind, like mine, that out of habit, much like a magnet, will hone in on what it's used to, what it's known and come to love.[4]

"Distracts me from idling"? Not only does that describe my negative thoughts, it also exemplifies their partner: the swollen analysis of anything harmful. After rereading the above passage, I realize that I was considering three determining concepts, all with their relative ends: growing in holiness, idling, and that which distracts me from idling.

---

[3] Saab: http://www.imdb.com/name/nm2265867/bio.

[4] Book #5, p. 2, 12-20-04.

Growing in holiness was the attention and action aimed at the good. Idleness was the lack of attention and action aimed at the good. If idling is the same thing as doing nothing, how could I be distracted from it? If I was actively consumed with evil, I wasn't idling. If I was actively consumed with good, I wasn't idling. So idling, according to my thoughts in 2004, was neither good nor evil. But I wasn't idling—I was being distracted from it. And since a distraction is a privation of something, which for me makes it less good, I was constantly preoccupied by what is worse than idling: "let alone growing in holiness."

Perhaps this example of room activity comes too soon, and maybe its logic is slightly flawed, but that analytical thought process consumed me for years and defined the nature of my room.

I imagine that there are many different kinds of rooms, many levels of consumption, and much moral measurement. We all, in one way or another, retreat to such a place. This book isn't intended to universalize every room experience but rather to describe the experience that was uniquely mine.

Saab admits his escape to a room as he

> made every effort to connect moments of pleasure in continuous succession in order to fabricate a sense of fake happiness. When the moments of pleasure fled, they took with them any lease I had on happiness. Like a junkie, I became addicted to my fix . . . they had become *needs*. My life was a constant stream of distraction.[5]

---

[5]   Gut Check, p. 34.

The odd difference between Saab's distracting experience and mine is that his solution was temporary happiness, fake although it was. I chose confusion and despair, both of which became so consuming that they separated me from reality, making me feel as though I was in a room. Isolation begot negative thoughts, and eventually I actually desired those negative thoughts. So instead of desiring happiness, I appreciated despondency.

Years ago, the psychological community coined the terms *psychotic* and *neurotic* and classified the mentally ill with those terms. The psychotic behaves in a way that alters reality completely. The neurotic only suffers from a partial alteration. The difference is that the psychotic escapes in an ultimate sense whereas the neurotic chooses when and how to escape.

Most psychotic people experience only one state of mind: a complete separation from reality—a complete separation in which there is no other state with which to reckon. The psychotic will usually lack awareness of what it's like to experience going in and out of the kind of mental room I created for myself.

This book mostly considers the neurotic by virtue of the room being, for me, not constant but rather a defense mechanism that temporarily ignored and actually prevented living the good life. Again, ignorance, in this sense, was actively denying what's real while trying to be unaware of that which was questionably (albeit loathingly) known as *good*.

Like many neurotics, I sought to prove that I possessed holiness despite my intermittent disbelief in its existence. Merton describes it perfectly when he says,

> The neurotic cannot help but self-consciously exploit his opportunities for spiritual "experience." He is compelled to do this to allay his anxiety and to justify his withdrawal from reality as a religious act. In actual fact his contemplation is a lie, an act of idolatry, and forms part of his private religion. For such men as this, the solitude and freedom of the contemplative life lead only to ruin. They are not capable of solitude because they are not strong enough in love.[6]

Merton is describing the beginnings of a created room before it goes bankrupt or, as he says, before it "leads only to ruin."

In the beginning I was compelled to believe in this self-developed room, which contained the illusion of truth and had round-the-clock vacancy. But the withdrawal from reality into seclusion proved to be harmful. And by virtue of the room being mostly interior, unlike substance abuse which is more exterior, makes the former more hidden—a structure that takes longer to unbuild. Merton agrees that the construction of a one-person room gives the illusion of truth when he suggests that

> it is very important to have competent guidance and instruction in the ways of contemplative prayer. Otherwise it will be almost impossible to avoid errors and obstacles.[7]

---

[6]   *The Inner Experience*, p. 112.

[7]   *The Inner Experience*, p. 95.

I said,

> One thing could be a universal observation: the fact that we all need help, we can't become good on our own, we can't grow on our own, we are not self-sufficient, self-retaining, self-existing. It's not good if we are wallowing, if we are wandering and pondering, if we are living in carelessness.[8]

"Wandering and pondering" was my room's method of separation. It advocated self-sufficiency and self-destruction as a way of life. And I often struggled to take heed of my own grace-filled insight found in that previous passage.

The following chapter shows how help from others was an option I never consented to; in fact I denied it. To deny something is, in a way, to separate from it. And this separation formed the habit of withdrawal; it was a move I made to receive the false peace of the room.

---

[8]   Book #5, p. 3, 12-20-04.

2

Prior to Room

The Experiential Cause

Having briefly described, in the previous chapter, what the room is, we can more effectively see what leads to it. By analogy, the room is that state of mind arrived at after certain experiential changes. But there must be an intervening factor for something to be changed and ill perceived. By this, I regard the emotions as the most common factor for why the recognition of object A is twisted and turned into an ill-perceived object B. Emotions influence our perceptions. In fact, they're so influential that they can cause an experience to be completely misinterpreted. That may sound delusional, and it can turn out to be, but strictly speaking a delusion is usually incurable whereas the imprint of a room isn't.

On 9-2-05, I had an insightful awareness of the ill-perceived thoughts that caused me to seek refuge in the room. I said,

My immature drive to be holy tells me that happiness
is not for me, and I am better off unhappy.[1]

---

[1]   Book #5, p. 45, 9-2-05.

An intervening emotion discouraged me from thinking I was worthy of happiness. When I wrote that passage, I thought happiness was an emotion that was "not for me" while simultaneously considering that idea to be an "immature drive." In other words, I thought I was being immature for thinking happiness was not for me. If only such moments remained long enough to begin, as Merton says,

> renouncing the illusory reality which created things acquire when they are seen only in their relation to our own selfish interests.[2]

My selfish interests are emotional; most selfish things are. Not remembering or correcting this "illusory reality" is what raised the tendency I had for exploring the room. Furthermore, the influence of my emotions was responsible for the dissociating fear which taught me to distrust people's words and actions. Distrust people until I identified them as condescending and threatening. Fortunately today that fear has dissipated due to people's love and partly due to psychiatric medication. But there will always be a vacant room in my mind, as in everyone's mind, offering the illusion of security similar to the old Hotel in California.

Apparently, an illusion can involve the absence of something we need, because for me, relating to and confiding in real people wasn't needed. It was how I took shelter; it was confiding in *The Forgotten Notes* that locked me away as seen in the following four quotes.

---

[2]   *Thoughts in Solitude*, p. 3.

I don't know what's going to happen to me. I feel hopeless, worthless. I don't want to keep trying. It's to tiring. Depression, what a scary space, what a scary place; it feels hellish. Like I'm stuck somewhere in a room and I'm too afraid to leave.[3] But my mind is still conditioned to think that (leaving) is not possible and not meant to be.[4]

I don't know what to do with my analytical mind when I read things I've written . . . I guess I need to focus on something stimulating, personal, and positive. That's what this writing is . . . but my thoughts are so fleeting.[5]

And I have an odd type of love for writing. I've been bothered by misleading thoughts concerning my purpose for writing, such as being motivated by the chance for self-recognition . . . [6]

It's odd that I imply a possible cause for entering such a debilitating room to be writing itself, while today I spend my time writing a book about it. It's odd too how I thought consuming my mind with such analytical thoughts meant I was being religious, pursuing an identity, and serving my purpose in life. My purpose: the one that I myself made, while thinking

---

[3]   Book #3, p. 83, 9-20-04.

[4]   Letter to sister (psychotherapist; no date).

[5]   Book #7, p. 16-17.

[6]   Book #2, p. 11, 4-16-03.

it was entirely given and destined from without, as if I've been sentenced to a life of despair for a good cause. And the thought would cross my mind that the despair sentence was to be fulfilled by writing a good memoir. But again, Merton hits the nail on the head when he says,

> It is curious to realize that those who most deride religious faith are precisely the ones who interpose between themselves and reality a screen of beliefs based on an illusion of self-interest and of passionate attachment. The fact that these beliefs seem, pragmatically, to "work" is all the more fatal a deception. What, in fact, is the fruit of their working? Largely a perversion of the objects manipulated by the exterior man, and the even greater perversion of man himself. Such belief springs from, and increases, man's inner alienation.[7]

This "interposed screen of beliefs" was a clever result of my interior struggle, which helped disguise the hardship involved in being me, because we're all different. And it was the differences about me that I longed to expose, but it was fear that kept me from doing so.

There's something good to be said about those who are authentically religious or contemplative. On the other hand, there's something else to be said about those who, despite the absence of such qualities, claim to possess them. And by claiming to possess them, run the risk of an inner conflict

---

[7] *The Inner Experience,* p. 20.

between who they claim to be and who they really are (a conflict via the emotions). And perhaps such is the case for everyone to a degree. In fact, if it is a universal experience, I'll consider that which might distinguish me from everyone else, how often and to what degree I've claimed to be who I'm not.

But first, it's important to know that it was my emotional misinterpretation of reality that agreed to be the person I didn't know I was claiming to be. It wasn't a person, persons, or religious institution that opened the door to my despair. In other words, it was my reluctance to accept my real self that interposed a fake me. But Nathaniel Hawthorne insists that this deception must be recognized at some point when he says,

> No man, for any considerable period of time, can wear one face to himself and another to the multitude without finally getting bewildered as to which may be the truth.[8]

I should've hoped to get bewildered by such deception, for not doing so meant falling prey to Screwtape's ploy, when he says,

> If he is a big enough fool you can get him to realize the character of the friends only while they are absent . . . If this succeeds, he can be induced to live, as I have known many humans live, for quite long

8   Nathaniel Hawthorne (as quoted by John Eldredge; *Wild at Heart,* p. 97).

periods, two parallel lives; he will not only appear to be, but actually be, a different man in each of the circles he frequents.[9]

After the created self toils with the real self for enough time, there's less chance to discover the ever-separating canyon between current beliefs and the real, reserving a secure habitation in the safe room. This is the room that promotes the false self and locks away the real one.

—

One summer, in my midtwenties, I went up to the Shrine of Divine Mercy for two nights to reflect, contemplate, and grow. I talked with the religious about life, I asked them questions, and I disclosed my ill-perceived beliefs. And it's funny how I thought I was holy and special by making a personal *retreat* to discuss my deep thoughts with them. And to some degree I was, but it's a shame because all I remember anyone saying to me, anyone at all, was a priest in these exact words: "You're quite the searcher." I don't remember any specific advice or guidance. All I could retain was being neutrally identified as a "searcher."

I was living in sin and making retreats to holy places. But hey, relax; I'm human, right? So yes, I do deserve to feel proud about making that trip. But honestly, that the trip was made solely to be recognized as being good and holy, and that's not at all how I felt. I had good intentions, and maybe

---

[9] *The Screwtape Letters,* p. 51-52.

I'm being overbearing, critical, or even scrupulous, but I was presenting my real self poorly and tried to live as though I was above ordinariness. So deep down I felt horrible behind the mask of a happy but hypocritical monk. And I'll save you the report of how that pilgrimage was full of sexual sin and destructive thoughts so Merton the Mystic can describe the all too common conflict.

> Tepidity, in which the soul is neither "hot or cold"—neither frankly loves nor frankly hates—is a state in which one rejects God and rejects the will of God while maintaining an exterior pretense of love for Him in order to keep out of trouble and save one's supposed self-respect. It is the condition that is soon arrived at by those who are habitually ungrateful for the graces of God . . . True gratitude and hypocrisy cannot exist together. They are totally incompatible. Gratitude of itself makes us sincere.[10]

Needless to say, Merton's wisdom regards gratitude and sincerity to be those virtues which avoid and detest recklessness. And at first, the lack of those virtues makes a lukewarm heart, or even an angry heart. But after that, like most things, the sky's the limit (for lack of a better direction).

Earlier, I disclosed how sometimes I was worse off than idling by actively denying the good or harming myself. Harming myself mentally because I was confused and trying

---

10 *Thoughts in Solitude*, p. 32-33.

to find a place to dwell. My lukewarm heart became cold, and my abode was the room before it was in people and God.

I was never totally committed to God. Tepidity formed the tendency I had for neglecting Him. The room was well aware that the battle between God and despair is that war which determines salvation. And what higher truth is there? God and people are the way.

But in the meantime, I called the shots, made the *wise* choices, and was becoming great. In this demonic room, I was safe and self-employed. But we're never completely self-employed, are we? There are always people to rely on whether, they are a group of clients or a single customer. And this seemingly empty room was run by the unseen corporate demons who were in it for the long haul—the haul that led to hell.

—

Eldredge says that in order to become healed, we need to "enter" our wound. Enter our wound as in understand it, but more specifically to live it. And in a way, that was my original intention. But eventually I was observing my wound in a room while analyzing other wounds that didn't have to exist, the ones I brought upon myself. I thought I'd be healed by writing about them. Now don't get me wrong: writing can certainly help us figure things out and make corrections. It's natural that to be healed from something, or resolve an issue, we need to know the problem, understand it, and find answers. That makes sense, right? Yes. So I furthered my introspection, wrote more, and became sincerely honest within . . . by myself. But The Mystic, even to this day, encourages me to break the room's deceptive design of writing within its walls when he says,

> Because of the superficial resemblance between contemplation and quietism, especially on paper, it has become customary and even perhaps necessary for one who writes on Christian mysticism to make sure that the reader does not confuse these two things.[11]

The idea here is to not confuse you but simply how I, the quietist, confused myself with being a contemplative. The overemphatic determination to solve my problems by thinking alone and writing in *The Forgotten Notes* became, while denying the help of others, a baited hook that reeled me to the front door.

In the beginning, I obliviously considered my intense passion for things to be the necessary proof for possessing truth, an illogical connection between them. In other words, I mistook the quietist passion of *The Forgotten Notes* for true contemplation. But for me, I'll consider quietism to be the lack of association with people, because my mind wasn't so much quiet as it was noisy and intense. It was isolated nonetheless, and so my mind thought it knew the truth, as if it could only be known alone. In other words, it became easier to think my beliefs were true simply because they were secret.

The intense focus on isolated self-help, contained entirely in *The Forgotten Notes*, was first directed at personal growth,

---

[11]   *The Inner Experience,* p. 103.

but again its aim was soon modified. My efforts became consumed by the deceptive propositions of a seemingly safe room. Eventually it was the proposal of a good-for-nothing existence lived outside the room that deceived me toward the birth of more complex problems.

> I picked up this pen with the plan to describe the type of despair I chose to experience tonight (*the type of despair I chose to experience? WHAT? That's not contemplation!*) . . . but I've done that so many times it's getting old, and frankly I'm happy to say it's getting a little pathetic. I'm well enough now to avoid the pity party.[12]

Or so I thought . . .

> Here we are again in *The Forgotten Notes* . . . writing when it's not good to. I am alive and breathing; that's a sign of hope, even though I'm deceived into thinking I shouldn't want hope, don't need it, and don't deserve it . . . I don't know what else to do.[13] God . . . why did you make me? . . . Can you please tell me soon? And why am I really writing this way? Is it narcissistic? Is it a way to be seen?[14]

---

[12] Book #8, p. 26, 3-20-07.

[13] Book #6, p. 29.

[14] Book #6, p. 44.

> The most comforting thought I know right now is
> writing in my journal, probably because it can't
> disagree with me or show me un-approval.[15] I am
> also calm because this way of expressing myself in
> a journal is a way of venting, a way for someone to
> know me because I am alone right now.[16]

"A way for someone to know me." That is true, despite
the fact that, until now, no one has read them. I suspect that
journaling was for me part of the room's RSVP, and perhaps
it still is, but I'm more balanced now; I don't care as much
as I did in the past when, for the better part of a decade, I
was miserably self-absorbed. It was as if I needed to explore
all possible reasons for why I was the way I was; I couldn't
just accept myself. I had to know. I had to know if fear and
other emotions were necessary conditions that contributed
to entering the room. I had to know whether my approach at
pursuing knowledge was healthy. And so began my obsessive
search.

> It seems as if the fear comes from a hurt and from
> a pain—traumatic in its effect. An effect that
> possesses intense emotions of feeling unloved
> and unwanted. And, as odd as it may sound, from
> this fear is born a new fear by the taste of feeling
> unwanted or unloved. And out of that fear is born

---

[15] Book #4, p. 16, 10-9-04.

[16] Book #4, p. 40, 11-12-04.

a rejecting denial that avoids the imperfect love
which began this flight.[17]

In other words, born by the familiarity of feeling unloved
and unwanted (whether I was or not) came a comfort and
security in those two feelings. But after such an introduction to
the supposed impossibility of love, what continued my flight
that led to the room?

Robert Bly describes two major routes that can be taken
when the mind can't handle what's real, leading to an avoidance
of it. One form of escaping he calls the "ascending route." The
other he calls the "depressed route." In his book *Iron John,*
Bly says,

> In our families, we can rise above the shame of
> having an alcoholic father by adding fuel secretly to
> our grandiose rocket, pulling away from the family,
> riding upward on that fuel. Or we can sink down
> into the shamed child, become him, be no one else,
> live in our secret unworthiness, lose our king, and
> become a slave. There is pleasure in becoming a
> slave. Then we can turn into an addict, and never
> be in charge of our own life, and shame ourselves
> further.[18]

We all get depressed, and we all have grandiose dreams,
but he's talking about serious defenses to pain including my

---

[17]   Book #9, p. 6, 3-15-08.

[18]   *Iron John*, p. 34.

defense against experiencing everyday insecurities. A defense by which I created a false self, allowing my real self to discover more confusion and wallow in it with the purpose of minimizing what was the mere present day's pain.

> I've got this irresistible drive to be different somehow, or to be labeled as "this type of person." To lift me up to some hall of fame or to lower me down six feet under. This drive is some type of overcompensation for the lack of love I have for myself. To acquire one of these *labels*, I would be committed to a category or a statistic, to a record of certain individuals who are *recognized*. I wouldn't be *just another person*. I would be remembered as great, as tragic, or as very special. As if I created myself and need to prove to the world that I did a good job.[19]

I saw no reason to simply feel sad, angry, or insecure as we all do. It's ironic, but I wanted to be *above* that, and thus worse off.

> It was all figured out, from the fame to the fortune to the death in my late twenties. That attitude was idolatrous, and it implied some super human qualities. There was an underlying confidence that was always self-crediting. The scary part is how for years this deception plagued me in too many aspects

---

[19] Book #8, p. 62, 9-22-07.

of life; and all the while I thought I was everyone's blessing: perfect in character and riding high to the highest bliss. When in reality I *(my real self)* was actually slowly sliding down a tunnel to a very dark chamber where I would soon be awakened to recognize the deceptive past and the long climb back out the tunnel, which now had big thorns growing out all sides. Harder yet, because of the intense deception that joyously brought me down the hole, the pseudo comfort and pleasure received from this empty room became just as hard to dismiss as the lonely fear felt in a crowded room.[20]

"Pseudo comfort and pleasure received from an empty room" is the familiarity factor found to accompany deception. That familiarity was the room's tool. It guided me to rely on it more than people, forming an altered reality, an altered self. My false self was the product and was displayed as a needless person who hoped that the craving for real help would never arise. Eldredge says,

You can never admit need, never admit brokenness. This is the story of the creation of that false self . . . . the two basic options. Men either overcompensate for their wound and become driven (violent men), or they shrink back and go passive (retreating men). Often it's an odd mixture of both.[21]

---

[20]   Book #4, p. 59, 12-13-04.

[21]   *Wild at Heart,* p. 73.

Both of them are determined to write their own history, to create a destiny or plan of life, even if that means avoiding any plan. In either case the mind makes uncontrolled plans. My neurotic mind's plan of operation was spiting reality through the distraction of a utopian self.

Saab emphasizes his driven ascending route when he says,

> My generation of twenty-somethings has given birth to the phrase "quarter-life crisis" because of the anxiety that comes with the knowledge that living the next fifty years of your life as Joe Normal before you die is a less-than-glamorous proposition.[22]

I didn't want a "less-than-glamorous" life, and this made-up room had a more enticing proposition.

> I've been writing the script of my own life for others to see for 5+ years now, and it seems like suicide is the perfect ending to my own story, and it seems like that's been the plan subconsciously for years.[23]

As Eldredge said above, "Often it's an odd mixture of both." It's obvious in my previous passage, made evident by the word "suicide," that the depressed route was my way. But based on other forgotten passages, there was a secret and euphoric mentality. After all, I was always split between

---

[22]   *Gut Check,* p. 108.

[23]   Book #5, p. 9-11, 1-2-05.

which one of my created faces would explain the reluctance
I had to be real; would it be the dead man, or would it be my
famous ink-filled-pen? And by the way, it is possible to write
a book and be normal at the same time; other people do it
every day. But even my awareness of such reluctant-to-be-real
explanations became incentives to make my life more desperate
and dramatic as when I said,

> Listen . . . this is complete nonsense! I'm writing a
> play! Even now, this seems to be part of the play. I
> know it is. And I can't stop. Amazing . . . Maybe I
> should stop writing and analyzing my life. But then
> I am confronted by the questions: What will I do?
> How will I live? It would make me go crazy to not
> feel or be crazy.[24]

I wasn't interested in living as "Joe Normal," and I didn't
want to pursue the good; it was too difficult. I was consumed
by the illusion that I shouldn't want and wasn't able to pursue
the good. The humility to recognize who I really was (a decent
person) took another spill because

> only with a certain sense of humility can a man see
> himself as he truly is, without taking comfort in the
> false notions of the person he *thinks* he is.[25]

---

[24]   Book #3, p. 63, 8-14-04.

[25]   *Gut Check,* p. 92.

"Without taking comfort in the false notions of the person he *thinks* he is." Saab says that well, although I was never comfortable with being the person I pretended to be. I've always been sensitive to living authentically despite my struggle to do so.

> I just now have realized that I am an outcast to my huge extended family, more or less. More less than more . . . I'm just not as happy-go-lucky as everyone else . . . I don't need to laugh and smile all the time, or comment on everything. I need to be myself, as happy as I can go. No more.[26]

"I need to be myself." That was an unkempt desire. Allow me to bore you by explaining what I, at that time, really understood as not being myself. Check this out, but read carefully because here's my efficient, abstract, dearth-of-nouns writing.

I remember (as the author of that quote) that not being myself referred to the supposed submissions I made to the pressures that I claimed to be against me. Claimed to be against me as if the happiness I saw in other people was an attacking temptation to be who I'm not, an alleged trap to which I frequently submitted. But the happiness I saw in other people wasn't against me; it was despised by me. In other words, happiness was viewed as that which I should deny. And I didn't even want to feel compelled toward pursuing happiness because it was too difficult to handle. And finally the intended conclusion of that passage: I will try to be as happy as other

---

[26] Book #1, p. 40, 8-31-02.

people pressure me to be "no more," as in, "I will not submit to what I can't handle or want."

Congratulations, you passed! It doesn't get more confusing than that. Anyway, the majority of that outlook has come and gone, so let's return to the story.

———

At age sixteen, I acquired a copy of Thomas Kempis's book *The Imitation of Christ* (a great read for those well disposed). But with no direction, guidance, or control, I read the book cover to cover. After quickly adopting what I thought it meant to live the hermit's lifestyle, I considered myself to be someone I wasn't, and I represented that false person poorly. Then I didn't listen to an uncle of mine when, during my face filled tears of discouragement, he said, "Jim, I think you're reading too many heavy books." I didn't want to be who I was because it wasn't fulfilling. So I continued reading, eventually began writing, and secretly crept onward to the room of enchantment, where supposedly I would find myself and learn about the truths of life. But in reality, that was the room's euphoric proposition leading me toward, as my sapient uncle advised against, "becoming above the world."

I couldn't describe this process better than The Mystic does in his following quote, so I won't try.

> If such an "I" one day hears about "contemplation,"
> he will perhaps set himself to "become a
> contemplative." That is, he will wish to admire,
> in himself, something called contemplation. And
> in order to see it, he will reflect on his alienated

self. He will make contemplative faces at himself like a child in front of a mirror. He will cultivate the contemplative look that seems appropriate to him and that he likes to see in himself. And the fact that his busy narcissism is turned within and feeds upon itself in stillness and secret love will make him believe that *his experience of himself is an experience of God* . . . He will assume varied attitudes, meditate on the inner significance of his own postures, and try to fabricate for himself a contemplative identity: and all the while there is nobody there. There is only an illusory, fictional "I" which seeks itself, struggles to create itself out of nothing, maintained in being by its own compulsion and the prisoner of his private illusion.[27]

That's a long quote, but it couldn't be explained more accurately. And it's funny that Merton mentions the child looking in the mirror, because I'll never forget how in my childhood home (about age seventeen), before high school's senior year, I practiced a slight smile in the mirror. That smile eventually became pasted on my face and led to an outgoing and popular graduating year. So basically my tears of discouragement, prior to the mirror's plastic surgery, were too tough to handle. Too tough to where I suppressed the tearful pain and resumed the creation of my false self and the reluctance I had to be real.

---

[27]   *The Inner Experience,* p. 5.

However, I had a few small warnings about this falsity when in my early twenties I attempted to explain, by negation, the true process of growth and the fallacy of adopting a smile.

> Wisdom isn't to be used as an escape, as a place we can go where we know it's safe. It is most useful, most helpful, and most effective when it hasn't just been adopted but rather acquired over time by patiently wanting to know why that is a truth.[28]

It's funny that ten years ago I considered wisdom itself to be a means for escape. But what I meant was the erroneous pursuit of such a gift, the claim of acquiring it effortlessly. The acquisition of wisdom through experience, guidance, and the virtues was what the room's alluring declaration claimed as ineffective. In fact, it proclaimed that personal separation was the answer to everything. Imagine that. Think you've got a problem? Well, forget about it. Wait, don't forget about it. Better yet, think about it over and over, all alone, and never tell it to anyone. I digress. In a basic sense, The Mystic differentiates between true and false when he says,

> When one is called into the darkness of contemplation, he is called to leave familiar and conventional patterns of thought and action and to judge by an entirely new and hidden criterion: by the unseen light of the Holy Spirit. This of course is, from a certain point of view, fraught with great

---

[28] Book #1, p. 64, 12-2-02.

risk. How does one know that he is guided by God and not by the devil? How does one distinguish between grace and illusion?[29]

The distinction could be made, in part, by how alone we actually are or how secretive we make our problems. So I wondered,

> Was I jumping the gun by portraying and living the life of a faithful Christian who I'm not? Have I skipped a whole lot of human and spiritual interaction? . . . One thing that's good out of all this is that I think I'm starting to recognize a need for that. But the fullness of that need seems so far away . . . (because) without hope, will it appear?[30]

"Will it appear?" Would I understand the necessity of interacting with people? Would I shed the narcissistic chains of being alone? Since then I have, but it was a tough thing to let go of. The room knew this and offered me doubt, hopelessness, and general distrust. So I signed the papers and fell further into its endlessly alluring despair . . .

---

[29] *The Inner Experience*, p. 76.

[30] Book #1, p. 24, 5-5-02.

3

The Haunting Allure

The desire for self-ruin—having the desire to annihilate yourself, to massacre your soul, your spirit, your health, and your attitude—is bad. This is hell. Or more accurately, it will lead to hell.[1]

The room's calling quietly rejected God; it tried to provide a sense of self-identity (a false one needless to say). Screwtape tells his nephew that man

> must not be allowed to suspect that he is now, however slowly, heading right away from the sun on a line which will carry him into the cold and dark of utmost space.[2]

---

[1] Book #4, p. 39, 11-7-04.

[2] *The Screwtape Letters*, p. 57.

That's interesting because here I said,

> I still am drawn to standing at the edge of existence . . .
> in the dark . . . alone with my back to the world.[3]
> My attraction to loneliness persists. My attraction to
> nothingness continues . . . Unknowingness is a huge
> attraction to me and always has been. Unknown and
> not in need. Self-sufficient, godless.[4]

What? "Drawn to standing at the edge of existence . . . My attraction to loneliness persists"? This draw, this attraction was the misleading allure of the room.

Unguided introspection designed the format of this room which I, in the following passage, called "a dream." I had good intentions for learning about this dream, but, again, that intention became disturbed as I focused on understanding it more and more.

> In the midst of this super spiritual episode, I thought
> to record it, possibly for the benefit of another soul
> someday or simply to collect my thoughts.[5] Rather
> than become depressed at whatever conclusions I
> may have unknowingly formed that contribute to
> the habit of self-defeat and self-destruction, I will
> remain in this state and let the song play, as if I'm
> in a dream, so as to dissect it and record anything

---

[3]   Book #6, p. 7.

[4]   Book #3, p. 49, 7-27-04.

[5]   Book #1, p. 71, 3-5-03.

that might be of help for the future, so when I return to that which I somehow choose to view as different from this, I will have that much more of an understanding.[6]

However,

life is not a problem to be solved; it is an adventure to be lived. That's the nature of it and has been since the beginning when God set the dangerous stage for this high-stakes drama and called the whole wild enterprise *good.*[7]

Real self-conquest is the conquest of ourselves not by ourselves but by the Holy Spirit. Self-conquest is really self-surrender.[8]

Because of my pride, self-surrender has been a challenge to this day. It has gotten much easier with time and God's grace, but, as they say, it's a process, and it's part of the out-of-room experience.

—

Screwtape's following passage exposes one of the room's tricks that lured me to residency. After all, why should I care

---

[6] Book #8, p. 82, 1-5-08.

[7] *Wild at Heart*, p. 200.

[8] *Thoughts in Solitude*, p. 18.

about my own interest, such as writing, when I should only be interested in what everyone else suggests: the supposed pressures of happiness that I claimed to be against me . . . Or so I once thought.

> The man who truly and disinterestedly enjoys any one thing in the world, for its own sake, and without caring two-pence what other people say about it, is by that very fact forearmed against some of our subtlest modes of attack. You should always try to make the patient abandon the people or food or books he really likes in favour of the "best" people, the "right" food, the "important" books.[9]

Although there may have been a best person, food, or book, that didn't mean I had to abandon all of my own interests. Recently, when I read that passage, it actually inspired me to continue writing despite Screwtape's preferred denial of doing what I really like. The preferred denial of what I really like, because he wants us to deny our passions when they're healthy and use them when they're not. And honestly, I can't help but wonder if the real Screwtape and Wormwood wish for me to continue or to stop writing this book. Then I wonder why I assume this passion of mine has enough importance to merit such an intense focus from these nonhuman beings. Answer: Perhaps because God's love for me is unlimited, as it is for everyone, and my passion is that gift from Him which Screwtape hopes to abolish. So the chances that this book will

---

[9]   *The Screwtape Letters*, p. 66.

serve God are now in His hands. After all, I'm just imposing my life on the general public hoping to be released, healed, and forgiven as if it was the eighth sacrament.

So I'll continue to write, despite any uncertainty, with hope that it will be for the good, as if I'm in that "blind state of grace" or taking that next step toward health. Who knows? Maybe this book will reach out to those who've made similar excursions from reality, and if so, well, that's great. Then this writing would be important enough for Screwtape to, as he says,

> Consider how we can retrieve this disaster. The great thing is to prevent his doing anything. As long as he does not convert it into action, it does not matter how much he thinks about this new repentance. Let the little brute wallow in it . . . Let him do anything but act. No amount of piety in his imagination and affections will harm us if we can keep it out of his will. As one of the humans has said, active habits are strengthened by repetition but passive ones are weakened. The more often he feels without acting, the less he will be able ever to act, and, in the long run, the less he will be able to feel.[10]

That's a brilliant C. S. Lewis passage. It's through good habits and good actions that I'm strengthened. A simple statement of belief may not be harmful, but then again, that

---

[10]   *The Screwtape Letters*, p. 66-67.

belief has the potential for stagnation. And thoughts alone won't save, but rather activity and contribution. After enough stagnation and inactivity, I advanced in my admiration of negativity. In 2005 I wrote,

> I'd rather withdraw from family and friends to remain in the ecstasy derived from whatever is happening while in this state. It comes back to this music; it's hard to think about not having this song play all day of every day. This is a preoccupation, a distraction.[11]

> I was just taken hold by the escaping power of music. I don't know the name of the song playing on the radio, but after it was over it left me frantically scanning the stations while driving to continue on the trip to this temporary bliss I would consider being in the middle of nowhere. But I am now at home writing about it with the *special* songs playing loud to soften the letdown of coming back to the silence and dreariness of reality.[12]

"Scanning the stations" is not the type of activity that Screwtape intends to discourage (in fact, scanning for loneliness and zoneliness was part of his corporate promotion). He intends to discourage the virtuous actions that give God glory, actions that I hadn't yet believed I was capable of.

---

[11] Book #5, p. 23, 2-12-05.

[12] Book #5, p. 42, 7-10-05.

These analytical and apparently musical preoccupations were my endeavor. I became fascinated with feelings of despondency and grandiosity. But I knew that all too well. Even while outside the room, I knew these preoccupations were detrimental. But they were familiar and I was inquisitive; it was the rhetorical rehashing of such discoveries that kept me away from reality because I was always able to describe and understand the blueness of my life in a different and more accomplished way. The problem then became following the room's counteractive rehashing insight even after understanding how it was evil.

> It's hard not to entertain the thrill involved with not living anymore—in community, society, or in any established institute involving people. It seems logical and really simple to think that peace of soul comes from the conviction and trust derived from a constant effort to keep stable our certainty of salvation when rested in Christ. But when deceived and manipulated, we see things upside down. If I've experienced this deception, miracle please! My mind wants to feed, but on what I don't know. I must know. I have trouble choosing what is right, because I have often felt convinced by this deception.[13]

"I have often felt convinced by this deception" Earlier you read about neurosis being not a constant or permanent state

---

[13]   Book #6, 12-24-06.

but rather a tendency which, given the right conditions, is agile enough to be swayed. Then in chapter two you read how I "picked up my pen to describe the type of despair I chose to experience" (a clear view of there being a problem). And Screwtape says that for him and his nephew, a human with this tendency makes everything easy.

> It all depends on whether your man is of the desponding type who can be tempted to despair, or wishful-thinking type who can be assured that all is well. The former type is getting rare among the humans. If your patient should happen to belong to it, everything is easy. You only got to keep him out of the way of experienced Christians (an easy task now-adays), to direct his attention to the appropriate passages in scripture, and then to set him to work on the desperate design of recovering his old feelings by sheer will-power, and the game is ours.[14]

And "recovering his old feelings by sheer will-power," means analyzing the feelings of my real self and dealing with them alone . . . and the game is theirs. In isolation, I am weak, so are we all. In isolation, there's too great a chance to be swayed: "the desponding type who can be tempted to despair . . ." Again, by the word tendency, I mean the natural inclination and the higher probability of not knowing what is happening, of not knowing what or who is tempting me.

---

[14] *The Screwtape Letters,* p. 45.

> I think it's the 26th. I'm not sure what is churning in my mind. But it's very familiar. The chapel was closed for some reason tonight so I couldn't sit there and learn. So I went away. And maybe I shouldn't have gone, but I still am . . . Despair is consuming. It's in every part of me. Sometimes, it covers me. It clouds me, it comforts me, it's . . . it is like a place . . . an escape . . . a . . . it's a . . . it's a release for my fears and anxieties. The only problem is it's hard to want to leave . . . it is hard to change the tune, the songs that provoke me . . . The security is part of the thrill.[15]

"It comforts me . . . it's hard to want to leave . . . part of the thrill." That's the result of a successful captivation. It was hard to want to leave because that meant surrender; that meant the thrill would be gone, as I described.

> Pride stands in the way of being accepted and affirmed normally. Pride is what desires a selfish self-defeat, a tragic happening in attempt to be known. I feel like I'm on a plain of nothingness. And the illness tells me that's what I should want . . . [16]

That's interesting. "Pride stands in the way of being accepted and affirmed normally." But why is that? Again, as a teenager, around the time of the mirror's smiling impression, I

---

[15] Book #8, p. 18, 2-26-07.

[16] Book #5, p. 23, 2-12-05.

became tired of fearing un-acceptance and thus, through pride, claimed to be someone I wasn't. But despite how happy or successful my pride appeared to be, my real self's suppressed existence took the loner complex a little too far. It rejected love the more it was needed, to the point where

> I feel like I am dying. Partly because I want to die, which is part of the problem my attitude. When will I convert? When will I give up? I can't go it alone. I am destined to fail by not giving up my life, my life to God. I must know and trust Him. I feel in serious need of direction. I've got to not want to slip back into the abyss of nothingness. It is a large, vast hole that has its attractions: being nowhere, alone without a purpose, not necessarily in pain like hell, but nothing like heaven. This is the drive to be nonexistent.[17]

The interesting thing about that drive, as seen in the next chapter, is that quite often I didn't thoroughly know what I was doing. After all, I never found the instructions on "how to become nonexistent." But perhaps I was better off not knowing that Thomas Aquinas, as quoted by Pieper, would consider such instructions to be those which signify

> a man renouncing the claim implicit in his human dignity. He does not want to be as God wants him to be, and that ultimately means that he does not

---

[17]   Book #5, p. 35, 5-1-05.

wish to be what he really, fundamentally, is. It is a "despairing refusal to be oneself" . . . the essence of acedia is the refusal to acquiesce in one's own being. [18]

I've never met another person who attempts this internal suicide for some misconceived good on a daily basis, but hopefully someday, if they're out there, I will.[19]

Hopefully if you're out there, you're getting help because

this is the mentality that would eventually lead to spiritual death and physical suicide. But I can't bear to live without that possibility. It's foreign and hurts to try and cry for help. But it is very much needed. I will go to my parents' house this evening after I leave the bookstore so I can be around real life. I don't want to, but I have to. I feel like I'm being haunted and taunted by demons. They want to take my soul and shred it up with their teeth. I can see and feel how they hate me because it makes me feel like everyone hates me, even my friends and family. There seem to be demons around me, and I want to get to know them and love them, but that's sick; I have no idea what that's all about. And God

---

[18] "Leisure the Basis of Culture," http://www.pc.maricopa.edu/ss/phi101/I/IA_Leisure_Basis.htm.

[19] Book #4, p. 39, 11-7-04.

is with me, it just doesn't feel like it. I can barely stand living. I wish to fall asleep and have angels carry me to heaven.[20]

While reading that passage written seven years ago, it sounds like nonsense; but they were my feelings, and I'm glad I wrote them down. And I know my family and my friends don't hate me. In fact, they love me very much, and I feel loved by them. But today, the love I feel from them sometimes makes me feel bad about how I, in the past, misinterpreted their love. Oh well, live 'n learn. And I'm still learning because I'm still living.

The reason for me knowing that I haven't lost all hope is because I'm still breathing, and because I'm sorting my mind out by journaling.[21]

One of the differences between writing about things and discussing them with others is that the pen and paper don't reciprocate. Unlike people, the paper couldn't advise me, console me, or love me. As for writing in the room, the only way I remembered what I experienced was by reflecting on what I wrote. And without such records, the entrance to the room might be entirely forgotten.

---

[20]   Book #5, p. 35, 5-1-05.

[21]   Book #8, p. 51, 8-27-07.

4

The Forgetful Entrance

The passages in this chapter expose my awareness of flirting with the room. In this sense, awareness will mean a partial remembrance which must, as Riechman says, presuppose the act of forgetting. Riechman, in his book Philosophy of the Human Person, discusses the act of forgetting when he says,

> Forgetting is not merely a simple non-knowing, or ignorance of something. Forgetting is closely related to knowing, and indeed in one sense it is a form of knowing, for we do not say we are forgetful of something without simultaneously implying that at one time we had knowledge of it. It is impossible, therefore, for me to say that I forget what I never knew. Forgetting is much more than merely being ignorant; it is a living testimony of my once having known.[1]

---

[1] *Philosophy of the Human Person*, p. 83.

It's necessary to understand Riechman's philosophy in order to completely understand *how* I claimed to forget things. But for now, we'll keep it simple and finish the story about what I'll call ignorance. After all, ignoring something is what this room was all about.

> I'm amazed at where I feel like I am most of the time, and in reality what I've led myself to believe. So arrogantly unconscious is my knowledge of self and life direction.[2] This mentality is seemingly good because it's all I've known for comfort. It's what I've been stooped into, it's what I've been trained to accomplish secretly: self-annihilation.[3]

"What I've been stooped into"? "Trained to accomplish"? By this alleged room? "Arrogantly unconscious" was my way of saying I refused to admit knowing that my intense introspection was damaging.

> The most fascinating thing about this twofold double reality life is how unnoticed it can become to my own self and how unaware I can be about its consequences. The longer this double life goes unnoticed, the more the problem perpetuates. This is simply because the reason I am in the room to

---

[2]   Book #4, p. 59, 12-13-04.

[3]   Book #4, p. 39, 11-7-04.

> begin with is because I have been deprived of that
> which the room doesn't want.[4]

"Been deprived of that which the room doesn't want" (i.e., the virtues, albeit deprived and rejected). By comparison to a normal person's lack of inclination to gravitate toward such a double life, there's nothing to forget about; there's an absent desire to confide in a room. This inclination was familiar and was a large part of why I overlooked entering most of the time. Furthermore, the clouded nature of entering the room served two purposes. First, it kept me inside, and second, it didn't allow me to think about why I should leave. But often enough, on paper anyway, I remembered what was happening.

> What might it mean if we suspect we've become
> too comfortable with the feeling of being content
> with despair and hopelessness? Convinced that an
> imagined destiny is known and created for ourselves
> by ourselves? Does that negate God?[5] Sometimes
> I go from thinking I do not want hope to thinking
> that I do, and then feeling afraid that there is no
> such thing.[6]

Here's a semi-complex summary of that passage: the "feeling afraid" that hope didn't exist was a good sign, as it implied the desire for courage to believe that it did. In other

---

[4]   Book #4, p. 43, 11-14-04.

[5]   Book #6, 12-24-06.

[6]   Book #7, p. 26.

words, my fear assumed its proper role, professed by hoping the feared object (despair) wasn't a characteristic of mine. And that useful fear would normally infer a courageous action which avoids the object. But courage would've taken effort, and effort is what I often lacked, resigning me further to the inactivity of the room.

> I've found that when I'm not actually thinking about it, the majority of my mind has come to terms with the idea that it's too late to get well, as if becoming a better person or being truly happy is not an option for me, and never has been.

That was obviously a bad sign, as it implied believing that there was no hope, and not wanting to even believe there might have been. "Come to terms with the idea" as in choosing to not remember that there is still time to get well. So the same entry continues.

> I sometimes recognize myself being comfortable with taking refuge in that degrading idea after attempting to believe differently. This might be a common or natural reaction to what seems unfamiliar, but these are ideas I should have known I wouldn't want to believe.[7]

---

[7] Letter to sister (psychotherapist; 11-1-07).

But again, in some way I did know. Merton describes this grievous belief as an exclusion, when he considers the "quietist."

> Christian contemplation is the perfection of love, and quietism is the exclusion of all love. Actually, it is the quintessence of selfishness, because the quietist encloses himself in his own shell and keeps himself in a torpor in order to shut out all the painful realities of life, which Christ would have us *face with faith and abandonment.*[8]

I always knew what needed to be done to live a healthy life: abandoning the false self and facing Christ with faith. But I had become too weak to think about the consequences of secretly retreating away from faith. There was no faith in the room. The room magnified the alleged impossibility of God's love, making me weaker. Weaker because my passions had come to understand the fact that, even though God was in my life, I could still ignore Him.

This next passage shows an awareness of the battle between my intellect and emotions when I wrote,

> It seems as though my understanding of living openly with Christ has been mistaken for being open to a life of random change or influence from wherever and whoever I see fit.[9]

---

[8]   *The Inner Experience,* p. 102.

[9]   Book #5, p. 12, 1-5-05.

As if a life of "random change," dictated by the room, could be responsible for real faith. As if that kind of open-mindedness could exist while maintaining and adhering to moral principles. But what is open-mindedness? It's a term used so flexibly. This may sound like an oxymoron, but I first experienced true open-mindedness when I was closed. In other words, when I was outside the room with the door closed, I wasn't open enough to learn without being "swayed" without being swayed into believing or doing something that was easier and less good. After all, "if you don't stand for something, you'll fall for anything." But in the beginning, I was so open that I fell for the room like a blind roofer. It swayed me toward living unwell. After all, the room was absolutely convinced that there was no absolute truth.

The following two passages actually display the forgetful process as an acute awareness of reality that was understood just before my weakness kept me from acting on it. (Sorry, that's how I like to write.)

> The reason why I'm writing now and probably half the time is not because I don't feel well, but because I don't feel perfect . . . At this exact day in my life, I only feel normal and comfortable when I'm "on the edge of existing," when out of fear I'm driven to find isolation. It has become such work to remain in the state of grace that I am in now and have been for three days. It has been most difficult, however,

> to bring myself back to reality, away from my idolatrous, glamorous, delusional way of living.[10]

> I have so much going, yet I'm in this room and every way out is now padlocked shut. No one is going to unlock them from the outside. Only I can, from the inside. But if I go out, I run the risk of everyone thinking so strangely of me. If I go out, I will be totally different, and I'll even go back into my room without knowing.[11]

If the separation process continued between my two selves, it could have become entirely forgotten. But again, by the in-and-out-of-room routine, I was reminded of the negativity that I "needed to write about" because of the previously recorded entries. And those entries weren't reread that often. But simply opening the journal to write reminded me about the task of sustaining my despair via some sort of habit or association. After all, the room didn't want me to forget about my "purpose" until I was totally committed. My purpose, as in being condemned to despair for a seemingly good cause. In other words, it was the habit of getting in touch with my neglected real self, who hadn't received any attention since his previously written entry, which would have me fully committed. It's akin to tapping into some sort of zone, a place where being alone meant being alive. This made the

---

[10]   Book #5, p. 12, 1-5-05.

[11]   Book #4, p. 20, 10-10-04.

experience more complex and more addictive. The following two-paragraph passage exemplifies this.

> Experiencing frustration, almost despair. I find myself wanting to be apart from all kinds of religion. But I seem to fear that state of existence, possibly from a conditioned past or sense of security. I only know God in one small way: that He exists. I am finding momentarily now that I need to detach myself for a while, but detach from what or who? I don't know. Hopefully I can live with myself and others enough to be courteous and polite and show some kind of human appreciation for being in their presence. After years of pain, I still find myself weighing and comparing the qualities of emptiness and loneliness with human interaction and *joy* . . . I suppose this is where I need great faith, perseverance, and patience. I could pray for it, but all of a sudden I don't feel like praying.

As I wrote earlier,

> Was I jumping the gun and portraying and living the life of a faithful Christian who I'm not? Have I skipped a whole lot of human and spiritual interaction? . . . I know God, and I trust in his compassion and mercy. But without hope, will it appear?[12]

---

[12] Book #1, p. 24, 5-5-02.

Remembering the virtues of faith, perseverance, and patience occurred mostly in writing because it was the journals that represented my real self and it was my false self who was represented pretentiously. When I was out in the community, I was a business owner who was engaged and owned a house; *The Forgotten Notes* knew me and the community knew someone else: the false self. So some of these forgotten passages have a hint of the virtues, but only inasmuch as they convinced me that I was healthy enough to keep hiding—a good excuse.

—

> Is it true that anything experienced with bitterness and confusion is an event not on the list or not in coordination with God's will?—Perhaps that's a leftover thought from the dead-end dream of living perfectly on earth. For regarding bitterness and confusion as in conflict with God's will, and therefore, to some degree immoral, is pretty much absurd. That's life. Those are the basic experiences and the inevitable regularities we all have to deal and come to terms with. How we deal with them and what we do about them is what defines ourselves as individuals with some sort of moral style.[13]

I would consider that to be a well-worded passage about the secrets of life which the room's selling agent certainly didn't disclose. Again, one of the reasons why I consider these

---

[13]   Book #1, p. 64, 12-2-02.

passages forgotten is because they were a rare reminder about my more positive ink-filled thoughts. For example, it occurred to me today that in the previous passage, "the dead-end dream of living perfectly on earth" is significant because it indicates the discouragement I must have felt with life not going my way. After all, who wouldn't be disappointed after really trying to become perfect?

Again, it was *The Forgotten Notes* that knew the "bitterly confused" person, and it was the community who knew the "trying to be perfect" person. In the community, it was the memory and familiarity of a mask which kept the composure my false self sought to maintain. In the room, it was the pleasure of fraternizing with my real self, whose depression needed to be fed and nurtured, as a baby boy needs his bottle. After enough room-written passages and enough altered living in the community, the separation from reality expanded, leaving much more to forget about and much more to ignore. In order to further ignore the positive things in life, I had to fix my mind on a greater sense of despondency. In other words, the more difficult it became to face the solutions, the more easy it became to embrace hopelessness..

> A very comfortable thought occurred to me about thirty minutes ago. It was this: "Death is always near." Well, this is depression. I'm happy to be alone with it. To live it. Take care of it. Record it. And ditch it when the time comes.[14]

---

[14]   Book #3, p. 80, 9-17-04.

And ditch it I would, as seen in the following passage's positive ambition.

> I need to be independent. I need to be myself. I need to do what I like to do. I like to pray and to think and to write. And I usually do all that on my own. I need to be confident about who I am, what I do, and what I like to do.[15]

> I feel now as if I want to busy myself with work, prayer, painting, guitar, hunting, and the pursuit of peace and happiness. But right now, for some strange reason, I don't feel too enthusiastic about doing things with others . . . Why?[16]

Well, right now I forget. It hurts too much to think of why I separated myself from others and how I may have hurt them. So I don't wonder why anymore; I just un-separate and unite myself with them.

> It's tough to gather good answers to the following questions. And it's tough to understand and think about them logically. Are we (you/me) really experiencing each moment? Are we taking in our surroundings as we live out our lives? Are we

---

[15] Book #1, p. 60, 10-11-02.

[16] Book #1, p. 60, 10-11-02.

soaking up everything we learn and handling what
God has given us as best as we can? Or do we sit
there, usually in some small form of ankle-biting
agony, hoping, wishing, and waiting to grow into a
stronger less depressive person?[17]

These questions are usually asked by those who seek
perfection, or at least holiness. This drive to be holy is good
in itself, but when we're hell-bent on achieving it without
help, arrogance and pride become accountable, not God.
The questions in that passage may have been productive had
I known how to ask them patiently. But I didn't. They were
questions asked just as quickly as they were dismissed and
forgotten. But at least the questions were positive. Although
it was written to psyche myself into thinking I was okay by
simply asking them (and not finding their answers), not all of
my secluded entries were superfluous sellouts.

Thank You, Lord, for this focused mentality. Help
me to obtain, keep, and make this consistent.
My thoughts early this morning concern the
disappointment we sometimes find with others and
ourselves and life as we search for the absolute,
the truth, You, the true light, the peace. And I am
curious now, and hope to find an answer someday
soon, whether this would be a deceitful or true
statement: One big thing we've got to realize in

---

this life is that we won't achieve perfection, but we can't stop trying.[18]

And I certainly didn't stop trying. I was out to dissect, understand, and explain everything about my life. Here the real part of me is trying to remember himself,

> I am alive still and writing to be seen . . . but the recognition I seek I suspect to be a product of that which is not me . . . And it's not me. No, it doesn't feel like me to think and write what I just wrote. But my right hand wrote it.[19]

> I am alive still. Usually a diary or a journal contains stories about specific experiences or events (a date, some drama, a job), but I write about my personal wellness or lack thereof. I suppose that's not bad.[20]

I often thought my journals were evil because writing was something that consumed my life. They were known only by me, and for that, the room's crippling character intensified. After all, secrets are meant to keep people out. And the very intention of my secrets were to make themselves easy to forget.

After consistently keeping people out of my life and my mind, it became harder to give up, to let God and others inside.

---

[18]   Book #1, p. 73, 3-8-03.

[19]   Book #6, p. 32.

[20]   Book #8, p. 9, 10-19-06.

I am still here with my pen in hand trying to conjure up some self-discovery to heighten my sense of self. If I were only able to give up and become myself in calm, serene contentedness, enough to be at peace with the human I am, who is good and imperfect.[21]

Once again, I feel compelled to write about my motives for writing. I sense at the previous moment that I am writing for others. But who should want to read about me when overall the depths of my life have been spent with ink on paper and with a million scattered thoughts?

The poor thought there is that because 'nobody cares,' I'll just keep the secrets close and continue to forget. So the speculative passage continues,

But God has always been with me somehow. So I must rise above the guise of false humility toward the truth and see that God, through my writing, just might be able to reach out to people and their deep, inquiring hearts.[22]

Perhaps admitting that this sort of journaling is an attempt to help others someday is the first step toward true humility, because in some way God is

---

[21]   Book #8, p. 26, 3-20-07.

[22]   Book #8, p. 43, 6-6-07.

inspiring me to write. I can rest that this journal is not evil.[23]

True humility recognizes the positive gifts of our lives. False humility, for me, denied their existence in order to avoid the task of cultivating them. I always wanted to help "reach out to people and their deep inquiring hearts" but always forgot I needed to first help myself. And no matter how hard I tried, I couldn't be helped alone. To use Maslow's terminology I now know I can't become *self-actualized* without God and other people.

> I'm talented, smart, and gifted. I don't want my drive to be great while simultaneously being for me. I want it to be for God! So when I see Jesus, He will have a big smile, open His arms, and I can run to Him as my Father, and so He can say, "Well done, my child, well done."[24]

But the heavenly thoughts were again put aside as the following entry, twenty-two days later, regressed to old analytical thoughts. Although the thoughts were insightful, they were also forgetful. There was no sign of a solution. They were a spiraling series of suspicions.

> With caution I open this pad to write, from fear that I might indulge in the ability I have to create and

---

[23]   Book #8, p. 41.

[24]   Book #8, p. 62, 9-22-07.

expound upon the unreality in my life. I suppose I'll never lose interest in being able to write romantically about life, but I do hope to be able to lose interest in writing romantically *and* going mad. So my thoughts just now are how I am unpleased with not who I am but rather who I think I am because of what I've chosen to believe.

The things I've chosen to believe, whether they are unconscious or not, have led me to act in accordance with those beliefs, and those actions have then, more or less, solidified the beliefs I didn't know I wouldn't want to have.

"Didn't know I wouldn't want to have." There I was claiming to have no part in acquiring the self-defeating, self-sentencing beliefs on purpose. But in a way, it was on purpose; the beliefs were so secret that I habitually forgot how I intended to acquire them. So again, in some way I did know. And ironically, the more unconscious the belief system became, the more it thoroughly consumed me. So the same entry continues.

It's apparent now that these concepts I didn't want to believe have consumed me for enough time to form the conclusion that it's not necessary, not right, or even wrong for me to believe otherwise. And that recognition is a basis or incentive, sometimes an attraction, to indulge in this pitiful frustration. But fortunately thinking about how I can describe that further is repulsing me. So I will continue to

write and to describe other avenues in my life as if
it is so vastly different from everyone else's; so my
unrevealed thoughts have led me to believe.[25]

"Unrevealed" as in the thoughts I "wasn't aware" of having,
which "led me to believe" in something as if it was from
outside myself. Again, forgetting that I intended to believe my
life was "so vastly different from everyone else's" when in fact
it probably wasn't, or at least didn't have to be.

But we all are specifically different. And small specific
differences can account for a diverse range of problems.
Problems that can get worse and problems that can get better.
For now, I'll write one more chapter describing what it was
like for me when they worsened.

---

[25]   Book #8, p. 67, 10-16-07.

5

The Intense Nature

The most intense part of living in the room has been recorded in *The Forgotten Notes*. The drama that's about to unfold is based on the belief that I must become more unhealthy and desperate. That distorted thought process took hold until it became natural to believe I was an unlovable and useless person who was not worthy of existence. I became a person who, for some important reason, had to become a nobody.

> I have been trained by my disordered and neurotic mind to seek isolation unprotected from evil thoughts and feelings of worthlessness for years.[1] It's very hard for me to think clearly, focus, and function normally. Either I'm worrying too much or thinking too much or something is wrong. I'm feeling unworthy of life. Out of place like I don't belong. But I'm comfortable in this. It feels like there's an identity attached to me.[2]

---

[1]   Book #4, p. 17, 10-9-04.

[2]   Book #5, p. 43, 7-17-05.

These are the concepts with which I was convinced.

> If I was to give way to my negative thinking, I might write something like this: I'm tired, I feel lost, and I don't want to do anything, not even sleep. I'd just like to cease existing. How can I be burdened so regularly by the desire to be nonexistent? I don't know. But it's real and I'm sure I'm not the only one.[3] It's so serious and so real I don't think I can honestly tell anyone about it, because it's all happening in my little room. No one else can see it really because it's my own place of habitual refuge.[4]

It was the secrets I held and my rejection of other people that lessened the chance for help. Earlier in the book, I mentioned how I formed an illogical connection between passion and truth, which led me to believe I possessed the latter. If the distorted passion of *The Forgotten Notes* wasn't kept secret, if anyone else knew about it, I felt as though it wouldn't be true. I would be exposed to alternative beliefs. I would be exposed to the alternative beliefs that I didn't want to know about and didn't want to be challenged by. The emotions that led me to form these illogical connections became dominating enough to where they convinced my rational *neutral* mind that they were true.

---

[3] Book #5, p. 19, 1-31-05.

[4] Book #4, p. 39, 11-7-04.

> I'm having neutral thoughts that say, *I should not*
> *have that fun. I should not try to maintain this*
> *confidence and happy living. It's not good for*
> *you to be this way, and it's not you.* So what do I
> believe?[5]

At this point, my estranged analysis and false beliefs became less emotional and more intellectual.

> I don't know what's happening. But nobody does.
> It's as if everyone is working together to help me
> (love? conspiracy?), or God is making me see
> firsthand and clearly how isolated and detached
> I've been from the good.[6]

That brings up an insightful thought: can paranoia be a distorted view of other people's emotions? Well, I think so. For example, when someone loves me, he will want me to feel it. And if that means pulling a few strings or going out of the way to influence my life, it's his loving intentions that matter; his emotion of love is trying to give itself to me. And I'm not referring to the demanding pressure of another person's imposed love (which, by the way, is a strain on the freedom to accept the real thing) but rather a patient, considerate, and unconditional love.

Although I have experienced this forceful offer of counterfeit love, most often that wasn't the case. Most often I received an

---

[5]   Book #4, p. 6, 10-2-04.

[6]   Book #7, 1-12-07.

invitation from real love. But it was this invitation from real love that I viewed as a conspiracy, doubting its existence. So by feeling conspired against, as if love wasn't real and as if I was being tricked, I rejected people, leading me further into isolation.

> I still feel so comfortable alone, and I'm lonely and afraid to be around others. I still feel like I might infect them with my sickness.[7]

"Infect them," as in bring them down or cause them problems. As a youth, like many of us, I was so inclined to believe that the problems of others were my fault. It follows then that because I believed I was at fault, how could I be loved emotionally? And eventually . . . how could love exist intellectually?

> Being in this room as I am, absorbed in this writing, involves a desire to stay here, an action resulting from fear. Being in this room can be likened to standing on the edge of the universe far away and simply watching the world function in its seemingly ordered way. Although, only wanting to do that some of the time, most of the time preferring to turn away and not watch, looking into nothingness, contemplating misery, and being content with the illusions of worthlessness.[8]

---

[7]   Book #2, p. 63, 5-12-04.

[8]   Book #4, p. 19, 10-9-03.

Those were my thoughts when the room's haunting allure became horrifically attractive. And eventually the allure was sought after because I was now an employee. My *responsibility* was accomplished by journaling. I was expressing myself in a way that relieved tension. It relieved the internal turmoil which had almost killed me. So when in need, I made the visit to my real self in *The Forgotten Notes*, talking to him and keeping him alive.

> When I'm being superficial for enough time, like we all can be, I feel the need to release the frustration that comes from the fear of being my true self. And I release it by indulging in negativity. By cutting through the superficiality and reaching the core of my pain, which I provoke and aggravate enough to arrive at an intense and seemingly thrilling form of despair. And in isolation for enough time, it builds and builds to the point where I do not want to let go. I want to go, go, and go, away, away, away. Where? Just away in my confused mind. Always in my mind, until I arrive at such a confused and desperate state that I freeze somehow, with complete inability to be a real man. Unable to function at all. Thank God I've only been there a few times, with enough hope to get out.[9]

I don't remember actually freezing, but I do remember feeling divided after truly considering my own existence.

---

[9]   Book #8, p. 21, 3-1-07.

After truly considering how I am me (a very odd but special experience).

———

Back to sixteen years old, while prematurely absorbing the monastic life through Thomas Kempis's book, I was also habitually in the sin of self-pleasure. Even if you, the reader, object and assert that masturbation and other fleshly actions are not sins, understand that they were for me because they contradicted the style of life I sought to live, per Kempis's literature. His book was strict and defined, ill suited for my unready mind. Eventually it intensified the level of self-doubt I already had, because I wasn't able to fit in his shoes. But I think it's important to clarify that Kempis's moral principles are valuable and are not to blame for my troubles. Rather, it was my previously formed vices that, in time, determined the level of my frustrated reactions. Had I been well prepared and called to the monastic life, I think the book would have helped.

There were times, however, when in a relaxed and balanced manner I rose above those despairing temptations, making it even easier to avoid much the same today.

> I am in the state of sanctifying grace! There is no doubt about that. That is the most reassuring thought I have at the moment. I will be myself! I am not afraid! God created me for a reason. I love Him and am thankful for His help. When I'm in the state of grace or if I'm not, the Devil tempts me to relapse to despair. Ignorance and weakness have given the

Devil a wide road to my soul. The sin, which my undeveloped emotional self got involved in, turned to a tremendously damaging addiction. And after years (10+), I was unfamiliar with everything except the overindulgence of the senses, mostly sexual flesh pleasures. The desperate, negative, hopeless mentality was born in my heart, mind, and soul, which led me to eventually feel more accepted and *at home* in the darkness. And the Devil has ploys to convince my mind that being in that darkness is what's best for me. I've even felt more (most) holy at times for avoiding human confrontation and ignoring the option of being with people who could possibly love me.[10]

Ignoring people and their love was the room's enticing solution, the one that originally seemed to make good sense but actually fostered death. The habit of ignorance is what made my secrets more hidden, even from my own mind. As usual, The Mystic describes this process perfectly.

But spiritual death is the sense of having separated myself from truth by complete inner falsity, from love by selfishness, from reality by trying to assert as real a will to nothingness. The sense of sin is, then, something ontological and immediate which does not spring from reflection on my own actions and comparison with a moral code. It springs

---

[10]   Book #5, p. 55, 8-21-06.

directly from the evil that is present in me: it tells me not merely that I have done wrong, but that I *am* wrong, through and through. That I am a false being. That I have destroyed myself. For sin is spiritual self-destruction. And the terrible thing is that though our body dies only once, our spirit, once dead, can still be killed over and over again. To be in sin and to continue sinning is to begin the life of a soul in hell, which is perpetual and perpetually repeated death.[11]

Wow! C'mon! Is he serious? Is he correct? I think he is. It's been this room experience that's led me to agree. And the majority of the forgotten passages provide evidence for my agreement.

I am comforted now by the silence and solitude of my own room. I feel free to think and do what I want. But I wonder: am I really trapped? Is my life so godless that I feel free when I'm in fact a slave to my disordered needs and thoughts? I love sitting here and feeling clueless, lost, hopeless, and in danger. But I know intellectually this is not a good way to be. And this disappoints me, because I'd have to lose my pride to find any solution. Satanic pride. I want to continue writing how I love the complexity I've made for myself, but I know it will only hinder me. Some strands of faith are pulling on

---

[11] *The Inner Experience,* p. 119.

me to disregard this entire habitual and seemingly good way of living, to abandon those ways and live the completely foreign and unattractive life. So I will go to bed and hopefully wake up alive to live another day.[12]

Again, Bly said, "There is pleasure in becoming a slave. Then we can turn into an addict." An addiction becomes consoling for one who is depressed. Its object then, becomes a source of security, a source of comfort, and eventually in the distorted sense, a source of love. We all need love to survive and false sources of it are plenty. The difference between love and slavery is that the former is real, and the latter is its distortion. But to the depressed addict, slavery is the most familiar route leading to comfort. The object of addiction, although irrelevant, can be anything. However, the more the addict escapes by pursuing these objects the more serious the sense of worthlessness becomes. Patrick Carnes, PhD, describes very well the mentality of the sex addict when he says,

> Addicts who regard themselves as "unworthy" survive in a secret world in which obsession blocks pain and loneliness and in which they are accountable to no one. Only the addicts know the whole truth. Each effort to quit that fails ads to an addict's sense of hopelessness. By keeping their obsessions secret, addicts, as well as family

---

[12] Book #5, p. 21, 2-3-05.

> members, maintain an illusionary sense of control
> and responsibility . . . Addicts and co addicts distrust
> other people, believing themselves to be unworthy
> and unlovable. Therefore they conclude that they
> cannot depend on others.[13]

"They conclude that they cannot depend on others." That's the illusion of self-sufficiency and control. Back to the possibility of viewing love through paranoid eyes, Carnes is saying there comes a time when love appears to be an attacking conspiracy. And it's odd to think that love, in its most basic sense, can become threatening to the point of denial. I was semiconscious of such a problem.

> Part of my problem is that I wish to not recognize
> how blessed and fortunate I am, with who I am,
> what I do, and all the great people I know.[14]

Looking back, it was fear and pride that pushed people away when they got too close. It was denying my worth as a person. By claiming to be worthless and not in need, I abandoned the opportunities I had to relate with others. Some say a vibe, some say an attitude; call it what you will, but I say it was more than both that told people I wanted to be left alone. And I didn't realize it, but the delusions I am being medically treated for, which have been happening since sometime in Book #4, are a result of this attitude.

---

[13]   *Out of the Shadows,* p. 171.

[14]   Book #3, p. 51, 7-29-04.

I suspect that, at that time, my conversations were a product of fearing a meaningful dialogue with real people. Consequently, by avoiding that dialogue, no one became close enough to where I'd fear his or her love. And eventually, through avoidance, no one became close enough for me to feel repulsed by how good his or her love really was (and that's more evil than it may sound). So, oddly enough, this issue manifested itself through incognizant and audible conversations with people when they were not around, a sort of compensatory activity that the docs have termed "unusual hallucinations." (I consider this psychobabble. Although necessary, it's a term that dispenses my meds.) The conversations were never much of a bother because I hardly knew they were happening. But today it takes less time to realize that I am not talking to an actual person. So I still dialogue, but fortunately I do the same with real people. I digress; it's just a remaining symptom of the room and a harmless state of mind.

—

Eldredge considers the resistance of love and dialogue with people to be a result of pride. In fact, he goes far enough to say that the refusal of love is a sin.

> Our sin is that stubborn part inside that wants, above all else, to be independent. There's a part of us fiercely committed to living in a way where we do not have to depend on anyone—especially God. Then culture comes along with figures like John Wayne and James Bond and all those other "real men," and the one thing they have in common is that

they are *loners,* they don't need anyone. We come
to believe deep in our hearts that needing anyone
for anything is a sort of weakness, a handicap.[15]

I'm sure he would consider the John Wayne/James Bond
complex to be an escape. It may involve being unimpressed
with ordinariness, or boredom with the simple life. It may
be chasing a pipe dream, moving from place to place or job
to job after becoming bored with the grass on one side, but
regardless of the reason, it's a sort of separation. According
to the ascending escaper, there's always something better,
something new, and something more interesting to occupy the
mind. For me, that separation was part of the thrill. I would
occupy my mind by analyzing new theories and inventing
a more despondent outlook on life. But the separation was
actually an ill use of my passions for the purpose of having
a purpose. I struggled to view God and other people as my
purpose because the loner complex was okay. It was popular,
accepted, and noble. Screwtape knew this and told his demon
nephew that

> the greatest triumph of all is to elevate this horror
> of the Same Old Thing into a philosophy so that
> nonsense in the intellect may reinforce corruption
> in the will . . . The Enemy loves platitudes. Of a
> proposed course of action He wants men, so far
> as I can see, to ask very simple questions; is it
> righteous? is it prudent? is it possible? Now if we

---

[15] *Wild at Heart*, p. 121-122.

can keep men asking 'Is it in accordance with the general movement of our time? is it progressive or reactionary? is this the way that History is going?' they will neglect the relevant questions.[16]

Basically, Screwtape is saying that his father tempts us to ask questions that don't consider morality. Earlier in Lewis's book, Screwtape says,

> Gratitude looks to the past and love to the present; fear, avarice, lust, and ambition look ahead . . . The sin, which is our contribution, looks forward[17]

> As a result, while their minds are buzzing in this vacuum, we have the better chance to slip in and bend them to the action we have decided on.

He then describes the future as containing those goals for which we ambitiously strive toward, which God would have us view with patience. Furthermore, Screwtape refers to futuristic thoughts as a condition which may lead us to sin (with emphasis on *may lead us to sin*). So it's our thoughts of the future which can sometimes be sought with selfish intentions. His entry continues.

> We have trained them to think of the Future as a promised land which favored heroes attain—not

---

[16]   *The Screwtape Letters,* p. 138-139.

[17]   Ibid., p. 76-77.

as something which everyone reaches at the rate of
sixty minutes an hour.[18]

"Sixty minutes an hour" is too slow! Even while writing this
book, I sometimes see a small part of me ambitiously striving
to conclude a story about his fallibly conjured up belief system
for a reckless reason. But today, thankfully, my intentions are
better than ever because they're patient.

It's important to consider how the pursuit of ambitiously
reckless goals was partly why I became locked in a room,
ambitiously reckless goals as in my focus on the *benefits* of
being negative. Although this book, for the most part, describes
my experience with negativity, it's unrealistic to say that it's
being reinforced while writing it. Unrealistic because it's now
about the past when my plans for the future represented little
more than death itself. In other words, today my future plans
are not aimed at a disconnection or a separation. Disconnection,
however, is still experienced today, but get this: I don't like it!

I've often wondered whether those previously conscious
plans of separation could ever turn into permanent states
of mind. Let's revisit modern-day psychobabble and
its diagnostic terms to make another distinction about
my out-of-room experience. Bota and Ricci describe a
psychosis as that which I consider to be a severely locked
room and perhaps a permanently locked one. In this article,
they regard the healthy act of discussion between people to
be a positive joining or aligning of minds, but

---

[18] *The Screwtape Letters,* p. 139.

in the preschizophrenia state that resonance, that alignment, is missing. The reverberation of that empathic connection is replaced by the "black hole" that swallows resonance and creates in the empathic examiner the frightful experience of being in the presence of someone whose humanity has now been hijacked, and only the opaqueness or strangeness of an "alien" remains as a sad reminder of a mind that was at one time like ours.[19]

That's a really nasty description of those who are so chemically challenged. I'd consider that passage to be a distinction between those less fortunate and myself. But at the climax of my despair, I certainly didn't leave much room for distinction, as said on 11-14-04.

The feeling attracted to, drawn to, or addicted to constantly residing in room, at its most intense times can be comfortably described this way: It's like a devilish cancer that eats you up from the inside out. Eventually this demon constantly tells you, "You can't go out there; you don't belong with them; you're different; you can't be with people; they don't even want you around. You'll just bring them down, you scum of the earth! Go back to your room—that's where you belong. There's nothing wrong with that; you're just different. Go on; you

---

[19]   Shamay-Tsoory, Tomer, Goldsher, Berger, and Aharon-Peretz, (2004), as quoted in Bota and Ricci, 2007, p. 319.

like to be alone anyways." Then the demon grabs hold of your insides, twists them so it hurts, and without recognizing it this pain puts a seemingly happy, but factually agonizing look on your face. And like a routine, you become so used to it. You're enslaved. And you hide out in this room all alone, away from people in fear, in isolation. You're addicted to it. It's too scary and foreign to go out. At this point, you've forgotten what it was like to be normal and on the outside with others. You're stuck in this vicious cycle, spiraling down, down, down into the bottomless pit of hell, and you thrive on this intensely chaotic concept of isolated nothingness.

"Isolated nothingness." Merton makes an important distinction when he questions the concept of "nothingness."

What does it mean to know and experience my own "nothingness?" It is not enough to turn away in disgust from my illusions and faults and mistakes, to separate myself from them as if they were not, and as if I were someone other than myself. This kind of self-annihilation is only a worse illusion, it is a pretended humility which, by saying "I am nothing" I mean in effect "I wish I were not what I am."[20]

I adopted the mentality in which my "pretended humility" made me appear fine. It was befitting to be a pretentiously

---

[20]   *Thoughts in Solitude*, p. 34-36.

humble person while hating myself. After all, how would I accomplish my future ambitions if I couldn't hide them behind a mask? In other words, if I didn't pretend to be humble through a false self, I'd have to be real, and that would attract too much attention to the reckless goals I wasn't ready to expose.

But even after times like those on 11-14-04 where my self-centered goals were materializing, I understood where there was light. So the forgotten passage continues.

> No matter how addicted and unperceived this room might be, there's always an invitation out. And there's always an understanding that there's something better, a life more fulfilling. And no matter how small or how infrequent this invitation to a new life might be, it's always there no matter who we are or the circumstances we're in. God's unconditional love will always call out to even those who are triple padlocked in their room. But the only way out is to unlock those locks ourselves, with the help of God and other people who are always somewhere for anyone as long as we look—as long as we desire to grow up and get out of room. The process most likely, depending on the time of our lodging, will be hard and painful. But to say the least, it'd be for the best![21]

---

[21] Book #4, p. 44, 11-14-04.

"Depending on the time of our lodging . . ." For me, depending on how long *I* chose to deny people, locking my real self in the room, and as Eldredge says, letting the "imposter" call the shots.

> From the place of our woundedness we construct a false self. We find a few gifts that work for us, and we try to live off them . . .

He then quotes another person's dilemma,

> The imposter within whispered, 'Brennan, don't ever be your real self anymore because nobody likes you as you are. Invent a new self that everybody will admire and nobody will know." . . . . The imposter is our plan for salvation.[22]

"The imposter is our plan for salvation." The imposter is the false self who acts irrationally. My community-driven false self blinded my real self from the light of truth by locking him in a dark room, a room of pessimistic despair. It was as if my doubly led life became competitive, aspiring toward the same goal: death. They became, as Freud would say, split. And at times, they weren't so much battling each other as they were together, hand in hand, working against the grace of God, contributing equally to the demise of my soul. That may sound overdramatic or superstitious, but I believe in spirits,

---

[22] *Wild at Heart,* p. 107.

immateriality, good and evil, and how all three are involved in every *out-of-room experience*.

It's unfortunate, this fact, and it's so true. I've come to know the Devil more than I know Jesus Christ. This is an accident. Somewhere in Scripture it is written, "Whoever is not for me is against me." And I in fact thought I was for Christ when I truly wasn't. I was trying to idle, trying to hover, when in fact hovering was declining, and with thick deception this was far from my mind. This is now painful to face. I am still closer to the Devil than I am to Christ, and this fact has recently been made known to me. But Christ, my true Father, knows me perfectly and loves me perfectly, and if I trust in Him then He promises me a beautiful life and a beautiful life in heaven with my family, with my friends, and with peace—not with fear, not with a bunch of chaotic circumstances or intense agony and love for every hellish feeling I've ever known. I've been in the state of grace for four days now, and I feel like I've come from the entrance gates of hell, having just stepped in, almost ready, and willing to burn in the beautiful flames of the idolatrous fires where I'd continue to resent everything that's against me and my desires because they're mine: my desires, me. I have a life. It is mine and nobody else's. I will do with it as I please. No more hell! No more![23]

---

[23] Book #5, p. 13, 1-6-05.

Basically, that passage is me resenting all the negative beliefs and intentions I've had (an appropriate emotional reaction to that which brought me down). And so begins the recognition and intention to think differently, believe in God's promises, and let my real self be known by other people. Eldredge says,

> In order to take a man into his wound, so that he can heal it and begin the release of the true self, God will thwart the false self. He will take away all that you've leaned upon to bring you life.[24]

He goes on saying,

> This is a very dangerous moment, when God seems set against everything that has meant life to us. Satan spies his opportunity, and leaps to accuse God in our hearts. *You see,* he says, *God is angry with you. He's disappointed in you. If he loved you he would make things smoother. He's not out for your best, you know.* The Enemy always tempts us back toward control, to recover and rebuild the false self. We must remember that it is out of love that God thwarts our imposter.[25]

God "thwarts our imposter" by exposing its lack of love. He lets us recognize.

---

[24]   *Wild at Heart,* p. 108.

[25]   *Wild at Heart,* p. 111.

6

The Recognition

I am recognizing the overwhelming feelings of
guilt, shame, and fear that I am doing so wrong.
That all I'm about, all I do, and all I think is wrong!
This demon who has conditioned my mind is a
genius. He has conquered enough situations and
circumstances to have manipulated my mind into
severe self-doubt and has satiated my desires for
the ultimate uncertainty.[1]

Was this recognition a result of God thwarting my false
self? Or was it my complicated real self trying to control and
distract me from His opportunities? Let's find out.

I am aware of the presence of their disguise;
coming in as neurotic thoughts. These demons have
taught me how attempting to have *control* can be
what seems to be a promising way of life. Control
in regards to approaching life with a self-sufficient

---

[1]   Book #5, p. 40, 6-5-05.

attitude by implementing a very limited recognition of how much I am loved by God, by others, and how much love I can reciprocate.[2]

The redundancy of my negative speculations indicates how locked away I'd become and the challenge involved with getting back out. In other words, I took my time before recognizing that God had to bring me "all" down, because I now think I was almost gone enough to be gone for good; no will power of my own would help.

It's been the unfortunate goal of mine to become as desperate and desolate as I became. Surprised now to still be alive, I am amazed at how each day is new. For 10+ years, I've sought to find my eventual death, partly from arrogance and partly from the idolatrous misconceptions I've had on the course of my own fate, with the deceived notion that I had my will conformed to God's.[3] It's obvious to me now that the direction of my journey is in the search for truth and understanding. Unfortunately, it has been a quest that thrives on intellectual dilemma and uncertainty and is uncomforted by conclusions, facts, and answers.[4]

---

[2]   Book #8, p. 31, 4-4-07.

[3]   Book #5, p. 20, 2-2-05.

[4]   Book #3, p. 66, 8-29-04.

Contrary to the real self expressed in the previous passage, the false self sought to affirm its own nature. The false self outside the room had something to prove. The false self was, as Conrad Baars would say, a self-affirmer. I tried to affirm myself as good based on how well I did things. And Saab, along with many others, shared a similar misconception.

> All my life I had been groomed to be as successful as possible, and my life was governed by the notion that my level of wealth and responsibility established my self-worth.[5]

My false self's quest for acceptance from the community was based on how well I could contribute to it. My other half, he was stuck in the room fearing exposure. Rather than accepting my imperfect real self as good for simply being me, a human, the room suggested that my false self must perfectly prove the value of my personhood by the quality of how I remodeled homes or designed someone's deck, or how well the guitar sounded while I played the blues.

> The difference between these two worlds, which I couldn't fully describe, is amazing. The best way to describe it would be reality and altered reality. Although separated from myself, I am alive and an individual person who is also separate from others. So I try to make some well-defined differences.[6]

---

[5]   *Gut Check*, p. 109.

[6]   Book #7, 1-12-07.

"Well-defined differences" as in the differences between me and others, which I never really defined but always thought were significant. What was defined, however, was how I became detached, needless, and afraid to be real. The help that other people offered was what I needed. And today, the love from other people has helped me become real. But again, at that time it wasn't viewed as love but rather an attack.

> Still, everyone is out to change me. Pride still. Everyone wants to help me.—Pride still. Emptiness. Complete nothingness. A strong desire to forget about everything and not help myself; I need no help.—Pride still. I don't want to be told what to do. Nobody likes to feel like there's something drastically wrong with him.[7]

I recognized these things and still decided not to believe something was wrong. I tried to deny and ignore it, as if being wrong and making mistakes didn't, or at least shouldn't, apply to me.

> When you look at the structure of the false self men tend to create, it always revolves around two themes: seizing upon some sort of competence and rejecting anything that cannot be controlled.
>
> That sort of commitment—the refusal to trust God and the reach for control—runs deep in every man.

---

[7]   Book #1, p. 27, 5-23-02.

Whyte talks about the difference between the false self's desire "to have power *over* experience, to control all events and consequences, and the soul's wish to have power *through* experience, *no matter what that may be.*" You literally sacrifice your soul and your true power when you insist on controlling things, like the guy Jesus talked about who thought he finally pulled it all off, built himself some really nice barns and died the same night. "What will it profit a man if he gains the whole world, and loses his own soul?" (Mark 8:36 NKJV). You can lose your soul, by the way, long before you die.[8]

Protecting the room's method became the focus of my attention. I recognized that the room led each half in the same breath, dismembering my real self and coercing my false self. I became familiar with this process making it very difficult to overcome. But overcoming this protective battle is still my intention, something I once described as

> a long, tedious process that requires day by day or even moment-by-moment concentration and focus to recover from an unhealthy addiction or from depression, or an addiction to depression. Both of those qualities have to be recognized as a problem before any kind of healing can take place.[9]

---

[8]   *Wild at Heart,* p. 203-204.

[9]   Book #1, p. 5, 7-10-99.

"Recognized as a problem . . ." As in made evident; an invitation for change. My real self's "addiction to depression" needed to be known and shown, allowing itself to emerge from the room and conquer the false self, which, believe it or not, is being accomplished while writing this book.

———

> Every once in a while, a certain number of thoughts and images come to mind, in which all the components of life seem to come together on a perfectly peaceful line. Almost as if the purest path or form of life is in sight. But after three minutes of pondering, thoughts of self-consciousness, temptations, and material possessions quickly rush in to cloud the heavenly thoughts.[10]

Temptations rush in as in the idea that I needed to think, decide, assert, and control everything to be me. However, The Mystic furthers his theory.

> Contradictions have always existed in the soul of man. But it is only when we prefer analysis to silence that they become a constant and insoluble problem. We are not meant to resolve all contradictions but to live with them and rise above them and see them

———

[10] Book #1, p. 5, 7-10-99.

in the light of exterior and objective values which
make them trivial by comparison.[11]

"Which make them trivial by comparison." Rather than
subjective values, which were made to accommodate my
selfish interests, the objective values are those which are still
correcting my false beliefs. Objective moral values are those
which I'll always consider to be universal and applicable to
everyone, *because* the saying "I'm absolutely sure there is no
absolute truth" doesn't hold a drop of water in my book. But I
digress. No more preaching.

The following passage returns to my real self's fear
of surrender. However infrequent it was, I recognized the
humiliation involved in abolishing the fraudulent false self
and exposing the real when I took myself for another ride.

> I can't believe I feel this way. My forehead is
> going to burst. I can't even look at anyone except
> my mother. She is always smiling. She's a saint.
> I am doing so well externally. I have so much
> going, yet I'm in this room and every way out is
> now padlocked shut in all possible areas. No one
> is going to unlock them from the outside . . . Only
> I can from the inside. But if I go out, I run the
> risk of everyone thinking so strangely of me. If I
> go out, I will be totally different, and I'll go back
> into my room without even knowing, by simply
> remembering subconsciously how to live as though

---

[11] *Thoughts in Solitude*, p. 80-81.

nothing is wrong. If I go out, everyone will know
something is wrong.

Nobody I know goes out like that!
Nobody![12]

The room's way of life eventually lost its appeal, as it
slowly became obvious that my real self wanted to emerge.
But it was humiliating because my false self now had a sense
of pride and

every man's deepest fear: to be exposed, to be found
out, to be discovered as an imposter, and not really
a man[13] . . . We are hiding, every last one of us. Well
aware that we, too, are not what we were meant to
be, desperately afraid of exposure, terrified of being
seen for what we are and *are not,* we have run off
into the bushes.[14]

I seem to still be in that little rut. I am recognizing
that the most comfortable place I know is in my
mind with this pad in silence and with no verbal
communication.[15]

---

[12] Book #4, p. 20, 10-10-04.

[13] *Wild at Heart,* p. 45.

[14] *Wild at Heart,* p. 52.

[15] Book #8, p. 35, 5-8-08.

I started to react to this recognition during my five-year period of psychotherapy with an APRN Franciscan Nun; I thank her for much of my recovery and health. Although recognition in this sense refers to our verbal interaction about the mere possibility of the room's belief systems, it was still a start. I wrote,

> Sister, There's been a few of your words that have stuck in my head since you said them: 'How much of you has come to terms with the notion that you are unloved and unable to love?' How much of me has come to terms with the idea that it's pointless/ hopeless to turn that notion around; to get rid of it; to believe deep down that it's not true. Have I learned to function so well with that belief that unbeknownst to others, and even myself, I still believe it's true? In other words, have I subconsciously come to terms/accepted that false notion to the point where it's understood? Where it's believed? Where it's viewed as normal for me? Where it's viewed as who I am? How I live? The way I shall remain? Is that something that I unknowingly understand?[16]

Pieper would say that prior to any healthy reaction, I didn't "agree with my own existence."[17] But of course I didn't choose to exist. I believe I was created. And to not agree with my own

---

[16]   Book #8, p. 39, 5-27-07.

[17]   "Leisure the Basis of Culture," p. 28.

existence would be to not fully understand that I didn't create myself. Again I said,

> As if I created myself and need to prove to the world
> that I did a good job.[18]

In other words, to really be in disagreement with my own existence, I must have, at some level, felt like I created myself. After all, it was harder to accept myself as a creation of God than to simply blame myself for my own poor creation and quit life altogether.

> My suspicion is, for the most part, that this drive
> is not a good thing for a couple reasons. First, it's
> mostly secret. Second, it implies that simply being
> a child of God who He created isn't enough.[19]

And that's certainly not true.

—

The out-of-room experience took time; it's still taking time. Like a lot of people, I have trust issues. For me they were clever and wormy.

> I've been living my life according to what other
> people think I should be doing. On the contrary, I've

---

[18]   Book #8, p. 62, 9-22-07.

[19]   Book #8, p. 62, 9-22-07.

also been avoiding doing what I think other people think I should be doing. Rebellion, basically. Has this avoidance been my pride's disguise to rebel against God? In other words, have I misplaced or projected God's calling on me to be from other people, making it easier to ignore?[20]

That's a great question. Who should we trust? How do we know if someone is acting on God's behalf or their own? If I actually took enough time to think about that question, I might have recognized that I could trust my family and friends as I do now. But at the time, it was much easier to simply trust my own beliefs and reject everything else. St. Augustine's following passage trumps all attempts I've made to unearth the result of my untrusting heart.

> My evil was loathsome, and I loved it; I was in love with my own ruin and rebellion. I did not love what I hoped to gain by rebellion; it was rebellion itself that I loved. Depraved in soul, I had leapt away from my firm foothold in you and cast myself to my destruction, seeking to gain nothing through my disgrace but disgrace alone.[21]

I can't say I was determined to rebel for rebellion's sake, simply because I was enthralled with the means by which I did rebel; the means whose aim was destruction and disgrace.

---

[20] Book #8, p. 66, 10-13-07.

[21] *Confessions,* Book 2, 2-4-9.

I recognized my trust issues and still listened to the room as it told me I only needed to trust myself.

> I'm attempting to appear, to someone someday, as if I am similar to the saints that we read about, like trying to imitate them! . . . But isn't that the goal we must all strive for!?! To be like the saints?!? After all, they are saints![22]

I believe in the saints and how they are worthy of trust and how each of them has virtues that are worthy of imitation. And a half year and forty pages later, I recognized the fallacy of trusting only myself.

> My attempts at imitating the saints in my own ways were erroneous, damaging, and secretive. To share it with most anyone else would seem to remove portions of the authenticity involved in this experience. And is that a bad sign? Or am I sensitive to the purity of/in truth?[23]

I was on to something there but hadn't yet recognized that illogical connection between passion and truth. In that passage, I said, "To share it with most anyone else would seem to remove portions of the authenticity . . ." In reality, what I meant was, "I'm afraid of the possibility that others have to challenge what I consider truth." In other words, "I don't trust

---

[22]   Book #8, p. 40, 6-3-07.

[23]   Book #8, p. 80, 12-31-07.

others." I was afraid of the possible love that others had to offer. After all, I was already shielding my real self behind the false one. And how could the room's shelter be maintained if other people knew about it?

But I was able to convince my real self, on many occasions, that the general contractor who owned a house and was engaged to a woman was really me, because I should protect the community from the desperate thoughts of my room, and, more to the point, to protect myself from the challenge of observing truth, trusting others, and the humiliation of rehab. My wounded interior self was locked away while the false self helped me appear normal (but not perfect as intended). The real self didn't talk, just wrote, leaving little chance for change. The more this happened, the more authentic it felt and the more it felt like my beliefs were true and would remain so as long as nobody else knew. But in reality, I was afraid and didn't want to be wrong, so for a little while longer I chose not to open up and relied on the room's *Forgotten Notes.* Yet The Mystic says,

> This is a most important discovery in the interior life. For the external self *fears* and recoils from what is beyond it and above it. It dreads the seeming emptiness and darkness of the interior self. The whole tragedy of "diversion" is precisely that it is a flight from all that is most real and immediate and genuine in ourselves. It is a flight from life and from experience—an attempt to put a veil of objects between the mind and its experience of itself.[24]

---

[24] *The Inner Experience*, p. 20.

"A veil of objects"? Perhaps a journal? Seriously, was my journaling something that protected my false self from remembering the thoughts and beliefs of the real self? Because how often would I remember my real self when it was only *The Forgotten Notes* that knew him. How often would anyone know about my pride and fear if they were only recorded on paper or discussed in an "unusual hallucination"? Why would my real self confide in people he didn't trust? Merton's passage continues.

> It is therefore a matter of great courage and spiritual energy to turn away from diversion and prepare to meet, face-to-face, that *immediate* experience of life which is intolerable to the exterior man. This is only possible when, by a gift of God (St. Thomas would say it was the Gift of Fear, or sacred awe) we are able to see our inner selves not as a vacuum but as an *infinite depth,* not as emptiness but as fullness.[25]

---

[25]   Ibid.

7

The Reaction

God must take it all away. This often happens at the start of our initiation journey. He thwarts our plan for salvation, he shatters the false self . . . Our plan for redemption is hard to let go of; it clings to our hearts like an octopus.[1]

By this being the case, I hope to humble myself enough with God's grace to recognize my humanity and start from scratch—start over, as it were. To let He who created me show me what true love is. To fall in love with understanding how and why my personal relationship with God and others is so completely and without question a necessity.

This, I trust, is happening now even as I write, as I raise my thoughts to God, and as I prepare for college starting in nine days.[2]

---

[1] *Wild at Heart,* p. 107.

[2] Book #8, p. 84, 1-5-08.

And it's still happening on and off, more on than off. And I found it important to remember that, as they say, life is a journey and not a destination.

> The thought process in regards to achieving attention by attempted suicide has come and gone . . . Negativity is deadly. Balance and virtue are my goals but feel like light years away. How do I relearn what to love? How do I recognize what I need to do? How do I shake the loving chains that hold me addicted to feelings of despair, hopelessness, and worthlessness? I am now to write down my suspected cure. Good works, by virtue, love and other people. How do I know this for sure? I don't. But my faith, whatever that means, tells me it's the only logical way, because my addiction, however twisted it may be, is selfish. So I've been inspired to write all this down, and I am in the state of grace, so I assume this to be an inspiration from God. But this I'm not certain of. Sister, can you help me? I'm frustrated. The conversion process is not easy. And if it weren't for my love of confusion, I'd hate it.[3]

---

[3]   Book #5, p. 7, 12-30-04.

Merton says,

> A man knows when he has found his vocation when he stops thinking about how to live and begins to live.[4]

My reaction time regarding Merton's insightful gem began slowly, but I'm happy with the progress made since my days when

> I want to spend an endless amount of time figuring myself out and learning about psychology and how it pertains to me. But I wonder if this is a hook I'm caught on while trying to leave my room. This excessive analytical work is no sign of a successful exit. The transition must be smooth and lasting in the out-of-room experience. The number of attempted exits may be huge—hundreds or possibly thousands, which may be an indication of how extreme a change the final transition would be from room to reality.[5]

Today I've learned to ignore what needs to be ignored: the room's allure and its thoughts inside. Ignore them because they are senseless and debilitating. I now know that

---

[4]   *Thoughts in Solitude,* p. 84.

[5]   Book #4, p. 33, 10-31-04.

I must choose God. I can live for Him. I can work for Him. I can pray by thought, by word, by deed, and by intentions each day. This is my only option. Every other option leads me to spiritual death. I've tried them and stood outside the gates of hell. Christ deserves my love. I am four feet away from an entity of God and am physically that close, but I see myself and feel like I'm miles away and just inching toward Him. For some reason, I cannot run.[6]

Eldredge says,

The only way to live in this adventure—with all its danger and unpredictability and immensely high stakes—is in an ongoing, intimate relationship with God. The control we so desperately crave is an illusion. Far better to give it up in exchange for God's offer of companionship, set aside stale formulas so that we might enter into an informal friendship.[7]

I see that now. I see that surrender involves mind, body, and spirit. St. Augustine confessed that,

---

[6]   Book #5, p. 14, 1-7-05.

[7]   *Wild at Heart,* p. 214.

How could I see it, since my eyes could see only as far as the body, and my mind only as far as illusion? I did not know that God is spirit.[8]

I am going to open my eyes fully someday soon. I'm almost there. Soon will be my out-of-room experience; I write that to be so. What happens will hopefully be recorded. This writing is the purest form of idolatry. I can't help but critique harshly about myself. It surely serves me as a release. As a fix. To a fix that contributes to the swelled ego within. I wonder now if everything about me will be stripped. Everything I felt that was so meaningful, so important, will be left behind.[9]

"Someday soon . . . will be left behind," to quote my own quote. But Eldredge says,

We simply accept the invitation to leave all that we've relied on and venture out with God. We can choose to do it ourselves, or we can wait for God to bring it all down.[10]

"Wait for God to bring it all down." In this case, "all" means the false sources of security and love that I've relied on and the tendency to withdrawal into seclusion hiding from

---

[8] *Confessions* Book 3, 3-7-12.

[9] Book #3, p. 67, 8-29-04.

[10] *Wild at Heart*, p. 112.

reality. "Bring it all down" as in having light shed on all the problems in a way that provokes a change. I think God shed his light on my false delusory self and inspired me to change.

> I'm tired of being a person pleaser. I don't care anymore. I don't want to care. I want to be unnoticed. I am not social and I don't care . . . I just want to be unconcerned. Quiet. Alone, but not completely alone.[11]

"Not completely alone"? Well, that's a start. That previous passage is an example of an extreme reaction to disliking my false self and disliking how weak my real self really was. Although that passage sounds negative, it's a normal reaction from being tired of an altered reality, tired of supporting the life of an imposter. Eldredge encourages men to be "real," to be honest, genuine, and courageous when he criticizes the person pleaser mentality.

> Yes, I know that Jesus told us to turn the other cheek. But we have really misused that verse. You cannot teach a boy to use his strength *by stripping him of it*. Jesus was able to retaliate, believe me. But he chose not to. And yet we suggest that a boy who is mocked, shamed before his fellows, stripped of all power and dignity should stay in that beaten place because Jesus wants him there? You will emasculate him for life. From that point on all will be passive

---

[11]   Book #1, p. 27, 5-23-02.

and fearful. He will grow up never knowing how to stand his ground, never knowing if he is a man indeed. Oh yes, he will be courteous, sweet even, deferential, minding all his manners. It may look moral, it may look like turning the other cheek, but it is merely *weakness*. You cannot turn a cheek you do not have. Our churches are full of such men.[12]

I was a people pleaser before trying to get comfortable in my own skin and before allowing my real self to make an appearance. My false self usually pretended to be good by offering polite gestures, poor generosity, and avoiding confrontation. I never stood up for my real self or wanted him to become a real man. He lacked the self-esteem and confidence needed to be one. But he knew that much and reacted to it.

I need to make myself an outline, something that I can refer to so I can stay positive and clear. A sheet that reads:

You are loved, believe it or not.

You are loved, want it that way or not.

You've been loved from your beginning until your end.

You must learn to love, want to or not.

You must learn to give, feel it or not.

You must think positively, uncomfortable about that or not.

You're not doomed; you are saved.

---

[12] *Wild at Heart,* p. 79.

You're not being manipulated; you're being helped.

Deep down, you're a simple and normal human who wants to do good.[13]

I actually printed that outline and kept it in my wallet. It seemed necessary for a despair junky, but it was still done alone. So it took time, but progress was made.

Something strange happened tonight. Good, but bad too. I opened all of my thoughts to a friend, and I now feel violated. But the reason I suspect to be this: all of this psyche work and the intense chaotic type of discoveries have been "my preciousness," my peace, my label, and my identity, because not many people know about it. *Hmmm.* I guess this experience is good because it's an opening up, a contribution toward getting out of my room.

But I am aggravated. Aggravated that this is affecting me this way. In its good way. This is because part of me doesn't want to get better. It wants to stay lost. It wants to be alone with pain, pity, confusion, and the love for their intensity.

As it is, that part of me is simply stuck, stuck in a room, and selfishly wants to stay because that's what I'm used to. That's what I've come to crave, know, and be happy at: to love in a twisted, sickly way.

---

[13]   Book #8, p. 35, 5-8-08.

Again, I convinced myself on many occasions that being *stuck in a room* was my only way, that the better ways, or the virtuous ways (which I knew existed), couldn't possibly be for me. So I suspect that the awareness in that passage was my reaction to being scared by talking to a real person (who wasn't a paid professional) about my deep thoughts, an expected reaction to such unfamiliar experiences. So the entry continues.

> I suspect the part of me that wants to heal is my longings for other people. In no other way, with these negative emotional feelings, would an isolation addict grow out of self and out of room as extreme as this . . . There's an interior call from God represented in so many people I know. [14]

It's not surprising to me that the back-and-forth/ in-and-out-of-room habit was revisited from my inability to leave the room cold turkey. Leaving the room was a process that involved a fear of exiting and a security of staying. But it also involved an excitement about exiting and a courage to stay out.

> I feel like I should stop writing. This writing is keeping me in my room. This day I was completely out! For hours! My God, I want to stay out! But I am still afraid.[15]

---

[14]   Book #5, p. 9-11, 1-2-05.

[15]   Book #5, p. 6, 2-15-05.

Jesus, where do I belong? I need to continue to put this instant gratification, this instant *love,* this heightened moment of personal awareness, behind me. I need to know that an even greater moment of personal awareness lies in wanting to die to myself to live for God. For knowing that I am one of His creations, He calls us to live for Him. Not as a chore, or strict responsibility, but for eternal peace and rest, without worry or frustration. And our capacity to live out that eternal peace grows the closer and more securely we live as Jesus taught.[16]

Those are some intense ambitions! At least they were healthy. Eventually, they became more balanced.

God, every day I hope to practice prayer, control, and patience, all to add to my progression of virtue, trust, and faith. So that these days of soft practice and obedient love for Your way of life will become radiant when need be. God, grant me this gift, so beautiful and authentic, to be experienced with such a humble and accurate view of Your will for me. Teach me, Lord, let me grow, bless me, give me Your gifts of virtue of the Holy Spirit so I may happily bring You glory.[17]

---

[16] Book #1, p. 44, 9-11-02.

[17] Book #1, p. 45, 9-15-02.

Those are nice thoughts and nice prayers; they're just like the ones recommended by all the *important* books and by the *best* people. They're the typical prayers on the back of every missal. But what about the deep dialogue with others about my pains and problems? What about not having to wear a peaceful mask in attempts to fool the community? In other words, what about being real? Forget posing for people, let alone God who already knows my real self. Forget about the artistic prayers of *The Forgotten Notes* which did little more than fool me into complacency.

Eventually I had to respect the needs of my real self and liberate him from the stifling false self. I had no problem with being honest in *The Forgotten Notes*, but being real and honest with other people took time due to my hesitancy. St. Augustine recognized his lingering habits when he wrote about attaining wisdom.

> I reviewed with agitation how much time had elapsed since, in my nineteenth year, I had begun my fervent quest for wisdom, making it my purpose to discover it and abandon all the empty hopes, all the deceitful delusions that my vain desires awoke in me. I was now some thirty years old, and still "stuck in the same mud" in my avid desire to enjoy things present, even though they tore me in so many directions; and all the time I said, "Wisdom? I will discover it tomorrow. It will appear before my eyes, and I will lay hold on it."[18]

---

[18] *Confessions* 6-10-17.

I am thirty-one years old now and

> I never honestly thought I'd be one of *those* people
> who gave their testimony about pride, sin, and
> conversion. But I am finding no other avenue
> but faith in Christ Jesus, an intimate relationship
> with Him, His mother, and the saints. I am going
> to try, from now on, to only write about faith and
> how necessary it is. To be objective seems to be an
> important thing.[19]

And objectivity is important, as is an "intimate relationship
with (Christ), His mother, and the saints." But again, I needed
to experience reality first. I needed to know how to relate, talk,
and learn from other people before I simply claim to love God
and pretend that I'm happy, before I memorize the prayers made
by the holy. After all, I am only human. We need relationships
to learn about virtue and to avoid the arduous task of getting
out of a room, the everlasting experience of my life.

---

[19]   Book #3, p. 63, 8-14-04.

Afterword

My Way Out

I'll never claim to be completely out of this mental room due to the fact that returning to reality takes time. The process will always involve those previous life events that are qualified to either hinder or help my present day's progress. But one thing's for sure: it will always get easier.

One of the biggest things I've learned is to not make a big deal and to not overanalyze everything—basically to relax. It's much easier now because I'm not alone in my head. I'm around people more and engaged in their lives, as they are with mine.

It was clear that, while writing *The Forgotten Notes*, I wasn't aware of the necessity for this balance. I was so eager to be heard.

> I am tempted to be lowered and tempted to seek sympathetic attitude. But I want to move out, out of room for good.[1] I can't believe what I'm leaving.

---

[1]   Book #4, p. 24, 10-13-04.

> This room I'm in, it's sickening. I hate it. But I can't
> go out and stay out. I don't know how.[2]

But I did know how, and I still do today, as seen in my involvement with friends and family. I am productive, not too analytical, and I am okay with my imperfect level of happiness. And it did help when I wrote about positive things.

> One of my fleeting goals is to be able to live while not feeling the need to receive recognition, praise, or approval from others, as if I was more than human, in order to understand my existence. I want to understand and agree with the truth that my existence is to love God and people. But since it was my immature and repetitious hand that just wrote that, it is yet I who understands it.[3]

"Yet I who understands it." Fully. I wanted fullness and perfection. I wanted to be in heaven. But I'm not; none of us are yet. We are humans who must get together, grow together, and give together. This is the purpose of life. That passage is full of good thoughts and desires. But if you've noticed, none of my present-day, narration involves such heavenly thoughts, because I'm not a hermit living in a religious order. Nor am I as spiritual as I thought I was. I'm a student who's stocking shelves at a retail chain for the purpose of being reintroduced

---

[2]   Book #4, p. 25, 10-20-04.

[3]   Book #8, p. 72, 12-7-07.

into the community, for the purpose of learning how to be real in the presence of people, and so far so good.

It's interesting now to see, despite its delusional pretext, how I analogically described this room as a place I was leaving, complete with its "door" and "lock." And this analogical view has contributed to the progress I've made since I started writing and thinking positively.

> I am stepping out. I am honestly happy with the progress I've made from page one of this book. I would consider myself, in the analogical sense, to have my door almost fully open. I am standing in the doorway, like a child, looking out, curiously experimenting, learning about living, talking, functioning, and trying to do that with minimal fear[4] . . . Right now I feel like a baby being born: speak/walk/eat and toilet ready. I'm waking up. I feel like somebody peeping through the bushes, coming out of a jungle, upon a beautiful city after being lost in the wilderness for years, and forgotten how to act.[5]

The positive play writing continues.

> I have been living outside the room now for four full days. It's bright and beautiful. I was consoled by my father not too long ago that someday soon

---

[4]   Book #3, p. 90, 9-29-04.

[5]   Book #1, p. 42, 9-5-02.

most all the burden would be lifted, and I hope this is just a taste of my positive progression. I wouldn't trade this conversion process, this disinfecting of the soul, this rebirth for anything.[6]

I still remember that conversation with my father, and his love comforts me. The attraction to the room's despondency still lingers today, but it is so much less than the past now that my real self is making the scene via God's grace. Via God's grace, I have courage and patience to relax and know that I am, like everybody else, an equal gift to humanity. And so my compliance to Him and His love began.

God, please show me as I pray now on paper for the light, for your light to understand who I am and what I was created for. But I suppose that before that, you would like me to be content with myself not really understanding what I was created for exactly.[7]

Exactly! "To be content with myself." Balance, patience, prudence. Every vice has a corrective virtue. I eventually realized that.

Christ, God, You do love me. You created me. I would not have feelings, thoughts, a body, a heart,

---

6   Book #5, p. 20, 2-2-05.

7   Book #8, p. 6, 9-23-06.

or an immortal soul if you didn't want me to. But You did want me to.[8]

I'm talented, smart, and gifted. I don't want my drive for greatness to be for me. I want it to be for God! So when I see Jesus, He will have a big smile and with open arms I can run to Him as my Father so He can say, "Well done, my child, well done."[9]

That was a nice thought, and get this: I still think it! I am still committed to not being consumed by the despair of an evil pride, the pride that rejects God and other people because it doesn't want to try, because it doesn't want to hope or believe in goodness. Positive thoughts were and still are the beginning of my journey to heaven instead of hell.

I am at peace. I am not alone in an empty room. The sorrowful mysteries have given me grace for I have been open to God's grace for 3+ weeks. Confiding in Jesus's heart and trusting Him is truly a gift when you're in the state of sanctifying grace. Everyone should know what this is about![10]

It's encouraging to know that those euphoric moments of peace are still something I desire. But now I also know that I won't be able to experience them all the time, day and night,

---

[8]   Book #8, p. 7, 9-28-06.

[9]   Book #8, p. 62, 9-22-07.

[10]   Book #5, p. 31, 3-15-05.

because I'm human. We're all human. The more time I spend with people, the more at peace I am and the quieter my mind becomes, because I'm also interested in them now. I've realized that I want people to give and people want me to give. In other words, love wants to give itself away; it wants to relate; it wants to confide and live with its reciprocating others.

> Tonight was special: the music, the repetitious music in my head stopped playing and I was in heaven as my deepest thoughts and intentions, and my real self, came out with another person. Never have I lived without worry, without fear of what another will think now that I've lost the fear of myself (the fear to expose my real self). Freedom, this was very unfamiliar. Talking was easy, special, and meaningful. Love is rich, pure, and it takes and it gives. Thank you, God![11]

More human interaction made the walls continue to crumble, making thoughts and writing more balanced and wholesome.

> I wish to write positively, even though it feels like I shouldn't try. As if writing again is a form of regression. But my committed effort to live positively is a sign to me that it will be good to write again, because I am thoughtfully balanced. My longing for heaven is astoundingly evident to

---

[11]   Book #5, p. 38, 5-16-05.

me. After months of control, today I've been at the tip edge of temptation to spiritual despair. But my friends were there with me, and God was with us men.

So I am becoming happy with life. My family and friends love me, and I've become part of a small community.[12]

God knows my motives, my conscience is being formed, my trust is developing, and the Devil is losing an ignorant follower who is sometimes afraid to leave. But I've already left. Recently there have been temptations, thoughts, or an option to now leave the light, the light of God that I have seemed to arrive at by grace, the light that I am deeply unfamiliar with, the light that I have once cleverly claimed to be in and superficially displayed. This spiritual battle must be seen, and be seen with a calm, patient understanding, and be tended to in balance.[13]

Again, balance has been the most reoccurring theme in my life to this day. Balance is that virtue giving me patience to overcome my vices, which allows the obsessive ambitions to slowly dissipate.

---

12 Book #5, p. 48, 2-6-06.

13 Book #5, p. 57, 8-26-06.

Although they may get tough, frustrating, and bothersome, no two moments are the same, and eighty years out of eternity is priceless. Let's live it well. Let's live it right.[14]

Surely someday I'll read this and smile . . . When I do . . . I'll write the smile with a date in pen right here__=)__ (#2 p. 17, 4-23-03; *smiley face inserted on 2-3-12*).

I want to someday soon finish *The Out-of-Room Experience* and record it officially and clearly to dedicate it to my two sisters.[15]

And that's what I've finally done. I love my two wonderful sisters, and they love me. And I know they also wish that anyone struggling with depression or despair will understand that,

no matter how addicted and unperceived this room might be, there's always an invitation out. And there's always an understanding that there's something better, a life more fulfilling. And no matter how small or how infrequent this invitation to a new life might be, it's always there no matter who we are or what circumstances we're in. God's unconditional love will always call out to even

---

[14]   Book #2, p. 21, 4-30-03.

[15]   Book #3, p. 81, 9-18-04.

those who are triple padlocked in their room. But the only way out is to unlock those locks ourselves, with the help of God and other people who are always somewhere for anyone as long as we look. And as long as we desire to grow up and get out of room. The process most likely, depending on the time of our lodging, will be hard and painful, but it's for the best![16]

"With the help of God and other people . . ." That's what being out of the room is all about: God and other people.

---

[16]   Book #4, p. 44, 11-14-04.

Acknowledgments

For help in working on this book, I would like to thank my English composition professor, Susan Krane, for the assignment of "reflecting on ourselves as a writer," which inspired me to finish this book. I would like to thank Dr. Angelyn Arden for her feedback on the psychological aspect of the book. And I would like to thank my father, James C. Mattingly, for the artistic front cover and his example of always being real and true. I would like to thank my mother, Cecilia Mattingly, for her constant unconditional love. And I would like to thank Daniel Caffrey for encouraging me to express myself from the heart.

Also, I want to thank all of my friends and relatives who've been so caring to me and each other. It was your example of virtue and your appreciation for me that literally began *The Out of Room Experience* and put me on the path to completing it analogically.

References

The Forgotten Notes

Book #1	5-01-1999 —	3-11-2003	75 pages
Book #2	3-13-2003 —	5-16-2004	69 pages
Book #3	5-17-2004 —	9-29-2004	90 pages
Book #4	10-01-2004 —	12-13-2004	60 pages
Book #5	12-17-2004 —	7-31-2006	62 pages
Book #6	12-02-2006 —	12-26-2006	45 pages
Book #7	12-31-2006 —	2-12-2007	45 pages
Book #8	9-16-2006 —	2-27-2007	85 pages
Book #9	1-08-2008 —	11-12-2008	13 pages

Augustine, S. (n.d.). *Confessions.* New York: Alfred A. Knopf.

Bly, R. (1992). *Iron John.* Vintage Books.

Bota, R. G., and Ricci, W. F. (2007). "Empathy as a Method of Identification of the Debut of the Prodrome of Schizophrenia." *Bulletin of the Menninger Clinic, 71*(4), 312-324.

Carnes, P. (2001). *Out of the Shadows* (3rd ed.). Center City, Minnesota: Hazelden.

Eldredge, J. (2001). *Wild at Heart.* Nashville: Thomas Nelson, Inc.

Lewis, C. S. (1942). *The Screwtape Letters.* New York: Harper Collins.

Merton, T. (1958). *Thoughts in Solitude.* New York: Farrar, Straus and Cudahy.

Merton, T. (2003). *The Inner Experience.* New York: Harper Collins.

Pieper, J. (1998). *Leisure the Basis of Culture.* South Bend, Indiana: St. Augustine's Press, Inc. http://www.pc.maricopa. edu/ss/phi101/I/IA_Leisure_Basis.htm

Reichmann, J. B. (1985). *Philosophy of the Human Person.* Illinois: Loyola Press.

Saab, T. (2008). *Gut Check.* Dallas: Spence. http://www.imdb. com/name/nm2265867/bio